Picnic

by
Barbara Swell

ISBN 9781883206642   Order No. NGB-850
Library of Congress Control Number: 2015937838
©2015 Native Ground Books & Music, Inc. Asheville, North Carolina
International copyright Secured. All Rights Reserved.

Introduction

If a ten year old kid that looks like this offers to pack you a surprise picnic lunch for your all-day outing, you might want to have a snack bar stashed in your back pocket. Just in case. This skinny youngster would be my mother, Nancy, circa 1937, and you won't believe her idea of a perfect picnic lunch back when this photo was made.

First, a little background: My mom's parents owned the grocery store in their single-stoplight town of Salem, West Virginia. They also tended a sizeable vegetable garden, so for the most part the Great Depression ignored their table. My grandmother could cook like nobody's business and her family of tall, big-boned folks could pack away some chicken pie and biscuits.

Nancy Smith Swell

Included in this family of prodigious eaters was my great grandfather, Cap'n Jack. The poor feller was about to get the shock of his picnic-lovin' life when, one fine summer day, he invites young Nancy to take a day hike to Sportsman's Lake for a swim and a lovely bite to eat. It's a hot day, they're dog-tired from their long hike and Nancy digs in her rucksack for the surprise picnic lunch she's packed for them. She proudly presents her paraffin paper-wrapped parcel to her grandfather, and he's wondering how can cold roast beef and thick slabs of Aunt Nell's pound cake possibly fit into that little package. He optimistically unfolds the paper to reveal young Nancy's

most beloved food of all. Bread crusts. Bless her heart, for days Mom had been stealthily hoarding the now-crunchy outtards from her salt-rising bread sandwiches for this special occasion.

I would like to tell you that good old Cap'n Jack was an amiable sport along about now, but I am not certain of that fact. Actually, he may have freaked out just a tad. Nevertheless, this was my mother's favorite picnic story and it's probably why I love picnics so much myself. We're a fun and quirky bunch, this family of mine, and the portable fare and projects I'm about to share with you are no exception.

Introduction

It's been on my mind to write a picnic cookbook for about a decade, ever since I ran across a copy of May Southworth's *The Motorist's Luncheon Book* while poking around a pile of time-worn cookbooks in the New York Public Library. Penned in 1923 – a time when motoring was more of a lifestyle than a method of transportation – the little book starts out with a chapter on *The Gypsy Trail,* and it's all about taking to the outdoors with your friends. I was hooked. May includes suggestions for foods that can be cooked over campfires or portable alcohol stoves and those that can be packed into handmade motor hampers and enjoyed cold or even hot from a new-fangled thermos bottle. She concludes her book with this enchanting blessing:

"In the spirit of good fellowship, to the enviable many who are bound to yield to the lure of the gypsy trail and feel the wild tingle of a hunger that simply must be appeased, Bon Voyage!"

Like May Southworth, I find myself enamoured with the merriment, conviviality and outdoorsyness of a picnic as much as the actual food. Sure, you'll find plenty of recipe suggestions in the pages that follow, but mostly I'm setting the scene for a memorable outing. One that contains an element of surprise that's outside the realm of your everyday life. Maybe it's a dandelion spritzer enjoyed by a mossy creek bank along with rustic oat crackers and your own deviled ham spread. Or a motor picnic that includes your homemade antique train case hamper that's filled with a jumble of vintage dishware and waxed paper-wrapped picnic fare.

Regardless of what's in your picnic basket, I hope you'll savor your moment outdoors and those you share it with. And to my 10-year-old mom, I'd like to say, "I'll gladly share a bread crust picnic with you any day!"

A DAY

A sunny day in early
June.
Made bright by recent rain,
Some happy children in a
field,
Weaving a daisy chain,
A wallet with a crust of
bread,
The sky above me blue,
The good brown road beneath
my feet–
And close beside me ~You.

Just You, Elizabeth Gordon, 1912

How To Use This Book

My favorite 19th century autograph rhyme goes like this:

When you are tired of life, and all its busy scenes,
just jump into the garden and hide behind the beans.

That's how I envision picnics ... a restorative break from the usual with companions or perhaps a solitary lunch amongst the beans. The food, the trappings, the perfect this or that matters little, really. Think of a picnic as a moment savored, more often than not outside, and with an element of the unexpected.

With that said, keep this in mind while reading these pages:

I know you're busy. This is not an uppity outing sort of book. My family's best picnic memories involve peanut butter and potato chip sandwiches, inner tubes and rambunctious mountain streams.

I'm aiming for you to include one special recipe, vintage prop or experience per picnic that's out of your usual repertoire. While I've included a few picnic classics, there are plenty of recipes for dishes that are a bit more free-spirited. If you don't have access to some of the items in this book, just swap out what you do have.

I learned to cook from rural Appalachian grandmothers who didn't measure with gadgets, and my own cooking is rather imprecise. These recipes contain lots of wiggle room. You'll need to sample as you go along and adjust to your liking. My tastes run toward less salty and sweet, so bear that in mind.

To increase the likelihood that you'll actually go out on that picnic, let fresh seasonal produce inspire your offerings rather than recipes. Shop your garden, farm stands or farmers markets for super fresh portable foods and enjoy as-is when possible.

And lastly ... I have way more picnic notions, recipes, projects and photos than could fit into this wee book. For more inspiration, color photos and tutorials, come visit me at www.logcabincooking.com.

Table of Contents

Picnic Particulars

Hooray! We're going on a picnic. Let's see, what sort shall it be?

> Solitary picnic under a nearby shade tree or a mossy creek bank
> Romantic picnic for two or a gathering of many
> Campfire or portable stove picnic
> A ramble in the woods or a walk on the beach picnic
> Backroads motor picnic
> Urban park bench or curbside box lunch picnic

You'll find suggestions for these kinds of picnics in this book and elsewhere, but the one I love most happens to be the "hurry-up" picnic. Not a fast food affair, mind you, but a non-fussy, spontaneous outing that's all about fun. I learned about hurry-up picnics from the June, 1920 edition of *American Cookery* Magazine:

"When a friend unexpectedly telephones, 'It's such a lovely afternoon, we're going to drive to the beach and have supper. We'll drive by for you in half an hour, and just bring along anything you happen to have in the pantry,' it is necessary to do some quick thinking. Having had a number of such experiences recently, I venture to offer some suggestions, for I have found these hurry-up outings give twice as much fun as those that are planned weeks ahead. One can't get very tired or worried over the cooking of a picnic lunch in half an hour. There isn't time!"

The authoress of the article goes on to suggest that we maintain a reserve picnic shelf in the pantry that is supplied with canned fruits and meats for sandwiches and salads. Instead of stocking up on canned goods, we'll be making use of our modern freezers to keep a store of outing-worthy, homemade portable foods as well as a few pantry staples that can be kept in your picnic basket. And, as always, farm and garden-fresh fruits and veggies will be the stars of the show.

"Its a picnic!"

Vintage Picnic Gizmos

We're about to discuss equipment, but just to get you in the mood, let's take a look at some make-do resourcefulness of yesteryear that I think you'll appreciate. First up is the 1948 *portable cooker on a tripod*, complete with a 6-prong wiener fork. This do-it-all picnic gizmo would be fun to make if you're handy that way.

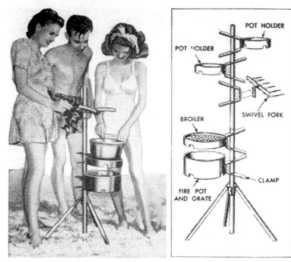

Portable Cooker Stands on Tripod

With a tripod base that holds it upright, an outdoor cooker has adjustable racks for holding a skillet, coffee pot and wieners. The six-pronged wiener fork toasts four at a time and swivels to cook both sides. Wood, charcoal or coke can be burned in the fire pot. The racks and fire pot have clamp-type brackets that lock in any position on the upright tube or can be removed entirely. For ease in carrying, the cooker packs into a compact kit, the long upright being made in two sections.

~Popular Mechanics October, 1948

With a dandy little portable oven like this vintage *Everhot* (pictured below), you can actually bake a cake at your next live-fire picnic. All you need is a source of bottom heat such as campfire embers or charcoal. Popular in the 1920s, these stoves were designed to sit on top of a wood cookstove or gas burner, but I can't resist taking mine to campfire picnics whenever I get the chance. The small ovens come equipped with

a rack and a door thermometer and bake like a home oven. Sort of. That's the make-do part of a vintage-inspired picnic that's so much fun!

If purchasing a vintage model, look for one with the original finish. For information on new camp ovens, see page 77.

Fresh plum cornmeal lemon cake bakes happily in a vintage portable Everhot oven.

Equipment

You don't need any special equipment for a happy picnic. And certainly, you don't want planning to squash the fun of a meal or snack taken outdoors on a whim. But if being prepared makes you more likely to picnic then, by golly, let's talk picnic baskets! Being rather picnic obsessed, I keep two vintage 1950s metal picnic baskets with wooden handles at the ready. One is empty and the other stores the equipment. When it's time for a picnic, I just put what's needed into the empty basket along with the food I'm taking. My little tin can hobo stove has its own carrier with room for sticks, tinder and matches.

No picnic for you Boo Boo. This bear was in our yard!

What's in Your Picnic Basket?
Here's what's in mine:

A small vintage tablecloth that doubles as a picnic blanket
Bottle opener
Folding sharp knife (I like Opinel knives)
Silverware (vintage as well as bamboo ware)
6 nesting plastic vintage picnic plates and matching cups
A stack of lunch-sized paper plates
Napkins (paper as well as a set I made from calico feedsacks)
Moist wipes
Small plastic bags for trash
Serving spoon
Spatula
Tiny wooden cutting board
5-inch cast iron skillet
1-quart vintage Revere Ware saucepan & lid
2 small vials of oil (olive and toasted walnut)
Tiny bottle of good balsamic vinegar
Tea bags and two pretty porcelain mugs
Itsy bitsy honey bear and unopened sample-sized jams
Spices in tiny glass jars: garlic herb salt, flaked sea salt, smoked paprika, hot pepper flakes, picnic pepper (page 16)

Equipment

The Picnic Hamper
Blanche Wade, *Youths Companion*, 1912

Into the hamper I may peep, for just a little minute.
To see the wondrous lot of things, that sister has put in it.
Bananas, cookies, jellies, cakes . . . at noon, oh how we'll scamper!
The really picnic part begins around the picnic hamper.

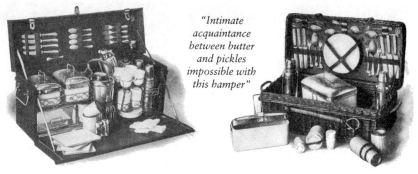

"Intimate acquaintance between butter and pickles impossible with this hamper"

Motor hampers can be procured either in leather or in wicker, and come in various shapes and sizes, with equally varying prices. They are very complete in every way. Some are fitted with a refrigerator compartment, and have a place in which to fit an alcohol lamp. They contain plates, cups, saucers, glasses, forks, knives, spoons, and two or three thermos bottles. ~Suburban Life, July 1911

Picnic hampers really did hit their stride in the early days of motoring just before the first World War. You can still find these well-outfitted hampers at antique markets for a tidy sum, but don't assume that the containers and thermos bottles are particularly food safe. Speaking of which, vintage picnicware is lots of fun, and I'm a big fan of decorative

tin picnic baskets, but do choose containers that are in good condition and give them a good wash before using. If the bottom of your tin basket is a little worn, just line it with a colorful dish towel.

My two 1950s tin picnic baskets with handy outing equipment

9

Handmade Picnic Baskets

W ayside picnic parks started popping up alongside what are now America's backroads in the late 1920s. Constructed in response to the pleas of early motorists for a tidy spot to rest and enjoy a bite to eat, many of these gems still exist and continue to enchant adventurous travelers much like yourself.

You'll be needing a sturdy and well-equipped road-trip picnic hamper that straps securely to the running board of your automobile for your summer backroad outings. Since we're at least 80 years too late to buy one, let's see what we can cobble together.

Humpback Bridge, Covington, Va

Picnic Hamper from a Vintage Suitcase
Popular Mechanics, August, 1922

Suitcase Made into Motor Picnic Kit

A suitcase can be made into a motor picnic kit without in the least preventing it from being used for its intended purpose. A piece of thin, tough wood, or a piece of wallboard, just large enough to fit snugly inside the top, is covered with denim or similar material, and suitable straps and pockets for holding the spoons, forks, plates and similar articles are sewed or tacked on, as shown. Glove snap fasteners, if they can be obtained, should be used for securing the straps. Strips of light wood are fitted into the body of the case to form compartments of the proper size for vacuum bottles, food boxes, drinking cups, and other articles, an individual compartment being provided for each. These partition strips are all fastened together, but not to the

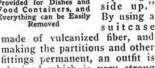

A Motor Picnic Kit in a Suitcase: Places are Provided for Dishes and Food Containers, and Everything can be Easily Removed

suitcase, so that they can be removed as a unit and the several strips prevented from becoming mislaid or lost. In this manner, the "legitimate" use of the suitcase is not interfered with, as everything can be easily removed. Such a lunch kit is carried just as any other suitcase when on the car, on the running board or trunk rack, due care being taken, of course, to see that the contents of the kit are kept "right side up." By using a suitcase made of vulcanized fiber, and making the partitions and other fittings permanent, an outfit is obtained which is very strong and practically indestructible. Genuine vulcanized fiber is very tough, and cannot easily be scratched and marred as can the ordinary leather case.—Walter C. Harris, Brooklyn, N. Y.

10

Handmade Picnic Baskets

In the spirit of a little 1922 *Popular Mechanics* make-do, I made use of what I had around the house plus a couple items purchased at a fabric store to transform this vintage marbled leather train case into a picnic hamper. It fits perfectly on the back seat floor of my Subaru, ever-ready for a roadside lunch.

After giving the leather innards a serious scrub, I cut a piece of cardboard to fit into the top of the case where a mirror once resided. The case happens to be 12 inches wide, so I taped a wooden ruler to the back of the cardboard for a brace before wrapping it with a clear contact paper-covered 1950s kitchen towel.

To secure my six-inch 1950s plastic picnic plates, I staple-gunned a strip of 1-inch wide elastic to the towel covered cardboard. The stapled elastic was unsightly, so I stuck a strip of fabric covered sticky-backed Velcro on top of it across the face of the cardboard case. Between the top and bottom layer of Velcro, I made gaps for flatware, a knife and a corkscrew. It's impossibly cute in color, for additional photos and detailed instructions, visit www.logcabincooking.com.

Materials used to make flatware holder on top of antique train case

Antique train case goes on a motor picnic

Handmade Picnic Baskets

Doctor Bag Picnic Basket

1947 Doctor Bag

Last spring, my daughter, Rita, and I were poking around an Atlanta antique shop looking for vintage picnic basket accessories, when she spied the booth of our dreams. Propped up on a pile of dusty old books sat a 1947 leather doctor bag in darn good condition. Rita is a nurse so she has an eye for such finds. The instrument compartments on the fold-out sides were just the right size for forks, napkins and cups. And wouldn't you know that right there beside the doctor bag sat a giant washtub filled with $2 monogrammed 1940s silver plated picnic-perfect flatware.

This fabulous and quirky medical bag has been on countless outings since its metamorphosis, and it's living proof that you can make a picnic basket out of anything! Here's how I outfitted it:

First, the bag got a good scrub using leather cleaner and conditioner. Always clean, line, and/or seal your antiques that will hold foodware. The instrument compartments and bag bottom needed a waterproof lining, so keeping to a 1940s theme, I rummaged in my attic and dis-

covered some colorful vintage printed chicken feedsacks. I wrapped the fabric around a piece of stiff plastic, then covered it with clear sticky contact paper. Then, I sewed through the layers to hold it all together, but you could duct tape the back just as easily.

Handmade Picnic Baskets

In full-out crafty mode, I made six smallish reversible napkins out of two other coordinating feedsacks (see resources, page 77 for more feedsack information). The napkins live in the doctor bag, as does a six-person place setting of vintage flatware and a

small retro tablecloth. I use the pill bottle leather loops to hold tiny salt, pepper and spice shakers. Of course.

Here's our Monday night picnic club enjoying a healthy doctor bag picnic. We shared:

- White wine with elderflower cordial ice cubes and strawberries
- Fresh garden veggies with buttermilk herb dressing dip
- Kale salad with honey mustard dressing and quinoa crunchies
- Salmon spread on a whole-grain baguette
- Blueberry, lime curd and Greek yogurt parfaits

Tin Can Hobo Stove

The gypsy sun is high all day, And the gypsy moon is bright,
But it's up again, and away, away. We're breaking camp tonight.

~Motorist's Luncheon Book, 1923

This little upcycled outside campstove is super lightweight and can bring a pot of water to boil in a few minutes with only a few twigs. I tote it to the garden to fry up fresh-plucked squash blossoms, or into the woods to make a cup of tea when the native orchids are in bloom.

The design was inspired by a 1980s rocket stove whose principles are pretty straightforward, especially if you're a physicist. Which, as you'll soon find out, I am not. For a more detailed tutorial, visit my log cabin website (www.logcabincooking.com).

You Will Need:

- ⚘ A permanent marker
- ⚘ Tin snips
- ⚘ Protective goggles and gloves
- ⚘ One #10 (one-gallon) can
- ⚘ One soup can (not pictured)
- ⚘ Three 22 oz. dog food cans (or you can use 28 oz. bean cans)
- ⚘ Wood ashes or Perlite for insulation
- ⚘ A grill grate or 6.5 inch round gas range grate (Frigidaire model #316055800 Burner Replacement Grates are $10)

To simplify this discussion ...

> The **big** can = the #10 can
> The 3 **medium** cans = the dog food/bean cans
> The **small** can = the soup can

Tin Can Hobo Stove

Let's Make The Stove:

Cut the top lid off of the large can, then do the same for only one of the medium cans. Set large lid aside. Using the lid of the medium can as a pattern, trace a circle on both cans as pictured. Be sure that the circles line up equal distance from the bottom. Using tin snips, cut holes in each can. Place the medium can in the larger can and line up the holes.

Remove the top and bottom lids of the two remaining medium cans. Thread one of them through both the outer large can into the inner medium can as pictured left. This is your wood chamber can where you will build your fire.

If you cut four slits in the can before you thread it through, you can fold tabs up as pictured left to help with the air flow. Maybe. That's a physics thing.

Get out the third medium can and remove the bottom third of the can with your tin snips. This will form the top of your inner chimney. Trim it to fit snugly inside the bottom inner vertical can so that it sits about an inch below the top of the big can.

Cover chimney cans with foil and fill gap with ashes or Pearlite for insulation. The chimney cans get HOT!

Cut a hole into the lid of the large can so that it fits nicely over the inner chimney can, covering the ashes. Cut and fold down a few tabs on the outer can to hold the lid in place as pictured left.

Lastly, you need a little wood shelf. Cut the soup can as pictured below, and place it into the opening of the wood chamber can. See stove on facing page.

Light your fire! Place a few sticks and some tinder on top of the little wood shelf. Light it, then poke and blow at it until it draws a fire. Cover your stove top with the round burner grate. Add twigs as needed.

15

Pantry Hints

Back 100 years ago, "wrinkles" and "kinks" were terms used for valuable information shared in the form of hints or practical suggestions. In that spirit, I share with you some handy make-ahead specialty foods and hints that will quickly add a bit of pizzazz to the humblest of picnics.

Apple Cider Syrup

When fresh cider is in season, slowly simmer it down to a syrup (four parts cider to one part syrup), and then water-bath can or freeze in little 4 oz. jam jars to use all year. Sweeten apple pies with the syrup, add a spoonful to salad dressings, or add a splash to mellow your hobo stove hot apple brandy toddy.

Traveler's Picnic Pepper

Grind up a blade of mace (the outer covering of a nutmeg) along with a tablespoon of black peppercorns in your food mill. Include a little pepper jar in your picnic basket to spiff up your outdoor meals.

Homemade Whole-Grain Mustard

Let easy-to-make homemade mustard be the star of your next outing. Inexpensive mustard seeds can be purchased in bulk at organic markets and Asian groceries. Serve with veggie sticks, cheese, cured meats and crusty artisan bread.

½ cup mustard seeds (spicy brown, milder yellow, or both)
½ cup apple cider vinegar
¼ cup apple cider, white wine, cognac or dark beer
½ - 1 tsp. salt, to taste
1 Tbsp. apple cider syrup, honey or maple syrup (**optional**)

Combine mustard seeds, vinegar and wine, then cover with plastic wrap and let sit 24 hours. Purée in food processor to a preferred consistency. Thin with water if too thick. Add salt and optional sweetener. Adjust the seasonings to suit you. Refrigerate up to two months.

Note: *For extra fun, try these flavor combinations:*
Cider vinegar + apple cider + apple cider syrup
White wine vinegar + white wine
Red wine or cider vinegar + dark malty beer + pinch allspice

Herb Garlic Salts

Fragrant garlic salt blends are so easy and fun to make, you will wonder how you ever survived without them! Sprinkle on vegetables, meats, olive oil for dipping, beans and soups. The possibilities are endless. You can get creative with your blends. Just be sure to keep the garlic to salt ratio the same. The better your ingredients, the better your blends, so start with flavorful fresh garlic and use a flaked Maldon or other coarse artisan sea salt if possible.

Ginger Garlic Salt: 4 medium garlic cloves, 4 Tbsp. flaked salt, 2 or 3 strips lemon zest, about 2 Tbsp. ginger chunks, fresh or dried chili to taste, few grindings black pepper.

Tuscan Herb Garlic Salt: 4 medium garlic cloves, 4 Tbsp. flaked salt, ½ cup total of fresh sage, rosemary, and parsley leaves.

Smoky Garlic Salt

Smoky Garlic Salt: 4 medium garlic cloves, 4 Tbsp. flaked (preferably smoked) salt, 1 Tbsp. smoked paprika, 1 tsp. chipotle powder or hot chili pepper to taste.

Celery Herb Garlic Salt: 4 medium garlic cloves, 4 Tbsp. flaked salt, handful of fresh chives, parsley and celery leaves, hot red pepper to taste.

To prepare:

Chop garlic and salt roughly. Add remaining ingredients and chop until well combined and finely minced. Sprinkle onto a parchment paper-lined cookie sheet and air dry a day or two until crumbly and completely dry. If it's being poky, then heat your oven up to no more than 170°, turn it off and let the garlic salt sit in there with the oven door closed. Don't bake the mixture! When completely dry, place salts in a festive glass jar. Makes a great gift.

Celery Herb Garlic Salt

Brown Butter (Caramelized Ghee)

You'd think that brown butter's nutty flavor would be praiseworthy enough, but if made in Italian Alpine farmer style, it also has high temperature cooking capabilities and needs no refrigeration. Perfect for picnic or campfire outings. According to Nonnas from the Valle d'Aosta region of northwestern Italy, timing is everything.

Brown butter from Turlen Alpeggio

First of all, in early summer, the beloved short-legged dairy cows travel from the valley up – and I do mean up – to the high Alpine pastures, called the Alpeggio, where they will remain until the fall. Rita (left) prefers the butter made from the sweet floral-scented cream that comes from cows who ate the first Alpine flowers of the season.

Wait, there's more. I've also heard that it's best if you do your brown butter making on the third day of the waning moon because everything that foams when cooking will froth less at this time.

Rita slices Fontina cheese

Now for the easy part. Let's start with one pound of good unsalted butter cut into 1-inch chunks. European butters are nice but use what you can find. Place butter chunks in a heavy-bottomed pan on lowest heat and do not stir. After fifteen minutes or so, it will foam; scrape it off and use it to season your dinner. Keep an eye on your butter now and when

it's amber and fragrant with a layer of brown bits on the bottom, take it off the heat. Don't let it burn. Strain through several layers of cheesecloth and place in a dishwasher-sanitized jar. For extra longevity, store in fridge when not on your outing.

Use caramelized ghee in baked goods, on veggies and in place of oil or butter when cooking.

Valle d'Aosta, Italy

Pantry Hints

Savory Flavored Butters

A snap to craft, flavored herb butters make fetching tea biscuit fillings and simple sandwich spreads. Freeze them in small logs, well wrapped in parchment and stored in a freezer bag. They'll thaw in your cooler come mealtime. A crunchy sea salt, such as Maldon or a Fleur de Sel is preferred if at hand, otherwise use kosher salt (I prefer Diamond Crystal). You can also just use salted butter if that's what you have. As a general rule, to ½ cup unsalted butter, add ¼ cup chopped herbs, ½ tsp. flaked or coarse salt (to taste) and half as much cracked pepper. The rest is up to you.

Salty butter for radish sandwiches:
Mix crunchy salt with softened butter and perhaps a tiny bit of chopped parsley. Spread onto a baguette and top with sliced radishes.

Tuscan herb butter for rocket stove pasta:
To softened butter, add chopped fresh rosemary, sage, garlic, grated Parmesan cheese, crunchy salt and pepper.

Nasturtium butter for tea biscuit spread:
To softened butter, add coarsely chopped nasturtium flowers along with a few of the round leaves, crunchy salt and pepper. Nasturtium butter is wonderful on fresh corn as well as steamed garden carrots.

Orange Powder

Such a simple way to add a hint of orange any time of year and it's more robust and a bit sweeter than zest. Orange powder is great with rhubarb, sprinkled on summer fruit as a garnish, even in your chili or hot cocoa mix. Makes a wonderful holiday gift, packaged in a decorative spice jar.

Cara Cara oranges make good powder

To make, place whole dried sliced oranges (page 37) in blender or food processor and grind until grainy but not powdered. Store in a glass jar with a tight fitting lid.

Beverages

As fun as it is to create these off-the-beaten-path seasonal flavorings for your picnic beverage, a simple garnish of fresh-plucked summer berries, lemon slice or mint is more than adequate to gussy up the plainest of picnic potations. For summer and spring, think bubbly, seasonal, refreshing. When poking around a campfire or campstove on a chilly fall evening, a fragrant, spiced steaming nip will surely warm your innards.

Kitchen Soldier Dandelion Spritzers

The 1918 edition of Good Housekeeping magazine offers war weary housewives a breather from the tedium of some serious food restrictions in the form of "drinks that clink for kitchen soldiers" recipes. They advise serving this cordial with wheatless cookies. Be forewarned, the delicate floral flavor of this dandelion "honey" will change forever how you view so-called weeds in your lawn. Pick the flowers in the late morning when the dew has evaporated.

Dandelion syrup/honey:

2 cups dandelion petals from about 150 dandelion flowers
2 cups boiling water
Up to ½ cup sugar (see note below)
Juice of a small organic lemon
1 organic orange, thinly sliced

Enlist a child to help with the dandelion gathering. Pinch the yellow petals from the flowers and then measure. Pour boiling water over petals and add the lemon juice and orange slices. Allow to cool, then pour mixture into a quart jar. Refrigerate overnight. Next day, strain and add sugar to the liquid. Simmer slowly until reduced by half. Pour syrup into a dishwasher-sanitized jar. Keep in the fridge up to two weeks or freeze into separate ice cubes.

To make a dandelion spritzer, add a tablespoon of dandelion blossom honey to each glass of Prosecco or other light white wine or seltzer. Garnish with lemon, bug-free dandelions and a mint sprig.

Note: The more sugar you add, the longer the syrup will last refrigerated. I prefer mine barely sweet, swapping a little honey for the sugar.

Beverages

Rhubarb Picnic Mojitos

If you're a rhubarb lover, keep this syrup close at hand for any number of great picnic uses. If you don't have rhubarb, you can substitute equal amounts of any summer berry.

White rum	Lime wedge
Fresh mint	Seltzer water
Rhubarb syrup (below)	

Minty rum: The evening before your picnic, combine 2 oz. white rum per picnicker with a few sprigs of fresh spearmint or peppermint. Refrigerate in a jar overnight.

Rhubarb syrup: Once made, syrup will keep in fridge two weeks, but rhubarb ice cubes, stored in freezer bags or jars, will last all summer. *(This amount of syrup will make 4 mojitos.)*

1 lb. red rhubarb stalks	½ lemon
2 cups water	4 Tbsp. sugar, or to taste

Dandelion cordial spritzer

Cut rhubarb into one-inch pieces and simmer with water until mushy. Drain through a fine mesh strainer, without mashing the pulp. Set the pulp aside for another use (such as sorbet, fruit leather, smoothie, etc.). Pour rhubarb juice back into the saucepan, adding enough water to make one cup liquid. Add a couple tablespoons sugar, more or less to your taste. Simmer until sugar dissolves, then add the lemon juice. Pour into a suitable jar and chill, or make into ice cubes.

To make mojitos at the picnic: Into each glass, add equal amounts of minty rum and rhubarb syrup, then fill with seltzer. Add a lime wedge, a sprig of mint and it's a party!

Beverages

Homemade Maraschino Cherry Wine Coolers

Not at all like the sort you purchase at the supermarket, once these bittersweet boozy cherries enter you life, they'll show up in more than just your wine coolers. Maraschino liqueur will put a fair dent in your wallet, but a little Weck jar of these exquisite cherries will make a mighty fine hostess or holiday gift once chilly weather sets in.

To prepare maraschino cherries: Pit fresh sour cherries such as Montmorency or whatever kind you can find at your local farm market and place them in a pretty jar. Warm up enough Maraschino liqueur to cover cherries ... don't boil, just warm. Pour over the cherries and refrigerate. You can also swap out brandy or rum for the Maraschino liqueur, but you'll need to dissolve sugar to taste in the warm liquor before pouring over the cherries.

Note: Add these cherries to pie, homemade marshmallows, vanilla ice cream, a Manhattan cocktail, brownies or fresh fruit kebabs.

To serve picnic-side: Into each glass, add a maraschino cherry plus a little of its liquid to seltzer, Prosecco, chilled white wine or rosé. Garnish with a slice of lime and a spring of mint.

A hand-stamped packet of mulling spices and a bottle of red wine makes a fine gift

Mini Mulling Packets for Cider or Red Wine

Packaged individually in glassine bags and tied with twine, mini mulling packets make great grown-up picnic party favors. Add to a quart of fresh cider or a bottle of red wine. Warm by the fire until fragrant, but don't let your beverage boil.

3 slices dried orange (page 37)
1 stick cinnamon
3 pieces either whole allspice or cloves

1 slice dried ginger (see note)
1 piece star anise (optional)

Note: To dry pretty ginger pieces, slice a fresh root very thinly longways and allow to dry at room temperature for a day or two. You can also use a dehydrator set at about 125°.

Beverages

Chocolate, Hot

Melt 3 squares of grated chocolate in ½ cup of hot water, add ¼ cup of sugar and 3 cups of milk, simmer 5 minutes, beating as soon as hot with a Dover egg beater. Add 1 teasp. of vanilla and 1 of sherry and a small piece of orange peel. Remove peel and when boiling again pour into the hot thermos bottle. Serve with a spoonful of cream in each cup. The cream may be carried in a separate bottle, and also more sugar.

Campfire Hot Chocolate Mix

A powdered version of Linda Hull Larned's classy "Chocolate, Hot" from her fun 1915 One Hundred Picnic Suggestions *cookbook. Serve with a dried orange slice and a splash of your favorite chocolate-loving liqueur, if you dare. Pssst ... how about adding a couple of those maraschino cherries on the facing page?*

⅓ cup cocoa powder
3 oz. bar of dark chocolate, grated
½ cup sugar

2 tsp. cornstarch
Pinch salt
1½ cup powdered milk

Give all a whirl in a food processor or just mix well in a bowl. Store in a glass jar until gone. To serve, mix 4 Tbsp. (or to taste) of mixture with a mug of boiling water. Top with a homemade marshmallow (page 65).

Curious ways to peel an orange, 1893

1897 advice from *Food, Home & Garden Magazine*

Eat fruit for breakfast. Eat fruit for luncheon. Avoid pastry. Shun muffins and crumpets and buttered toast. Eat wholemeal bread. Decline potatoes if they are served more than once a day. Do not drink tea or coffee. Walk four miles every day. Take a bath every day. Wash the face every night in warm water. Sleep eight hours a night.

Starters AND Snacks

D elight your picnic-mates with a festive beverage and a specially packaged or prepared nibble to set the mood for the day's moveable feast.

Chocolate Orange Picnic Popcorn

Buttered popcorn tossed with your homemade flavor sprinkles, packed individually in waxed paper bags. What's not to love? Staple a flower or a fresh herb sprig to each bag. Mixes are saltless because you may find other uses for them such as chocolate orange molé chili or perhaps a smoky iron pot pork roast.

Pop ¼ cup popcorn kernels in 2 Tbsp. oil. If air-popped, toss with one Tbsp. melted butter. While popcorn is hot, add 2 Tbsp. of the chocolate orange powder mix. Salt to taste.

Chocolate Orange Powder Mix
1 Tbsp. cocoa powder
4 Tbsp. (1 oz.) grated bittersweet chocolate
2 Tbsp. powdered orange (page 19) or
    1 Tbsp. fresh orange zest

Note: During citrus season, collect zest from oranges you are about to eat or cook with. Store in a little jar in freezer for summer seasoning.

South of the Border Molé Popcorn Seasoning
To the chocolate orange powder above, add:
¼-½ tsp. ancho or other chili powder (adjust to desired heat)
¼ tsp. cinnamon
Salt to taste

Popcorn Patties *When Mother Lets Us Cook,* 1908
Boil together 1 cup of sugar and ½ cupful of molasses, until thick and waxy when a few drops are tested in cold water. Stir into this a quart of popped corn. Drop heaping spoonfuls onto a buttered plate. Set in a cold place to harden before eating.

Starters AND Snacks

Brown Butter Sage Leaf "Sandwiches"

Served straight out of the pan by their tails, you and yours will be delighted that such a simple snack can taste so good. I often bring my hobo tin can rocket stove to the garden and make a batch of these little sandwiches on weeding and tending breaks. Be sure to use a firm cheese that stays put when melted. Feel free to experiment with other fillings such as smashed chickpeas and roasted peppers (see photo below).

> Fresh sage leaves, at least 4 per person, stems on
> Brown butter or regular butter
> Firm, aged dry cheese like Parmesan, Romano, Asiago
> Salt to taste

Pick large leaves of your favorite sage. I love easy-to-grow Berggarten's voluptuous, rounded leaves for this appetizer. Heat up your little camp-stove skillet along with a pat of butter. Place a thin slice of cheese on half of each large sage leaf and fold over. If your leaves are small, just make a two-leaf sandwich. Cook until light brown and crispy on each side. Sprinkle with a bit of salt, if needed.

Roasted pepper and smashed chickpea sage leaves

Crispy sage leaf served on a rock

Crunchy Garden Radish Nibbles

Choose young radishes whose greens are super fresh looking. Long skinny French breakfast radishes are ideal, but any will do. Wash well and snip off the tails, keeping the leaves on. Take them to the picnic whole. You'll also need to bring a folding knife, some unsalted butter and crunchy salt. If you have time, add the salt to softened butter at home, and refrigerate in a small container. Once at the picnic, keep leaves on and slice radishes longways, just enough to poke some salty butter between the two halves. Serve by the stem.

Starters AND Snacks

Deviled Eggs

Somebody's gotta bring them to the picnic. Why not you?

To cook eggs:
Boiled: Place cold eggs in enough water to cover by an inch. Bring to a boil, then cover pan and remove from heat. Let them stand 12 minutes, then drain and crack them in a couple places. Let eggs sit in ice water until you can handle. Peel by running a spoon under the membrane, fat end first. Also, boiling them a day or two in advance and refrigerating them uncracked makes for more peelable eggs.

Steamed: Place eggs in a steamer basket over simmering water and steam, lid-on, for 12-15 minutes, then soak in cold water a few minutes. Even the freshest eggs will peel easily using this method, but practice making them this way before the picnic to get the cooking time correct for your taste.

Slice 6 hard-cooked eggs in half, remove the yolks and smash well with:
>3 Tbsp. mayonnaise
>1 tsp. mustard
>1 tsp. or less vinegar or sweet pickle juice
>Salt and pepper to taste

Add-ins or ons: Cooked bacon, fresh dill or chives, grated cheddar cheese, sweet pickles or hot, roasted peppers, olives, pimento cheese, deviled ham and, pretty much, any old thing you can think of!

If you're not the official deviled egg person and don't have an bona fide deviled egg carrier, just assemble the eggs at the picnic. Bring empty egg halves in a covered dish and put the creamy filling in a plastic zip bag. Once at the picnic, cut the tip off the bag and pass it to each guest to fill their own, along with a teensy jar of paprika or other garnishes. Or, how about this handy tip from my friend Marti ... stuff eggs at home, put facing sides back together and wrap each whole stuffed egg individually in a piece of waxed paper.

Starters  Snacks

Personal Guacamole Bowls

Are you looking for that one festive element to make your unfussy picnic special? Well then, these do-it-yourself guacamole bowls could be it. They never, ever, fail to impress. The lime wedge is essential, the rest of the add-ins are up to you.

½ ripe avocado per person (you'll halve them at the picnic)
Small wedge of fresh lime per person
Add-ins: finely chopped cilantro, minced onion, jalapeno, hot
    sauce, salsa, a dab of sour cream
1 sturdy fork per picnicker
Veggie sticks or chips for dipping

At the picnic, slice each avocado in half and remove the pit by giving it a good whack with your knife. Give it a twist then dislodge the pit from your knife with the help of a nearby stick or rock. Hand an avocado half to each guest along with a fork and a lime wedge and whatever pre-chopped add-ins you carried with you. Smash guacamole innards with forks right in the shells and pass those dippers.

Gianluca and Annie enjoy a mossy log forest picnic

Spreads AND Dips

A hint of smoke and a bit of char will add charm and authenticity to a host of picnic foods enjoyed in a rustic outdoor setting. These spreads are no exception.

Pimento Cheese Spread

If you're not a big fan of mayo-laden fare, then you might prefer this sturdier version of a popular southern cheese-and-pepper sandwich spread. Before you start hollering that I've messed with tradition, note that pimento cheese was originally a mixture of Neufchatel cheese and canned pimento peppers that had been sent through a food mill. In the early 1900s, it was sold in blocks to be used as a spread for crackers or sandwiches, with a little mayonnaise and chives along for the ride.

> 8 oz. sharp cheddar cheese, grated
> 2 oz. Neufchatel cream cheese
> 4 Tbsp. mayonnaise
> 1 large roasted red pepper, chopped
> 1 Tbsp. finely minced onion, or chopped chives (optional)
> Pickle juice to taste (from sweet pickles or pickled peppers)

Optional:
> ¼ tsp. good smoked paprika
> Few shakes hot chili pepper or smoked chipotle pepper powder

Combine all ingredients and add enough pickle or pepper juice until spread is a consistency that you like. Taste to adjust the seasoning.

Spreads and Dips

Hummus in a Veggie Forest

1½ cups cooked chickpeas (¾ cup dried, then
cooked or a 15oz. can)
2 Tbsp. lemon juice
4 Tbsp. tahini
1 garlic clove, smashed
1-2 Tbsp. chickpea broth or water
Salt to taste
Good olive oil to drizzle

If using canned chickpeas, reserve two tablespoons of the broth, then drain. If using dried, soak chickpeas for 12 hours, then cook in water to cover until tender. Salt toward end of cooking. Let them cool, then drain and reserve two tablespoons of the broth. Blend chickpeas, lemon juice, tahini and garlic well in food processor until smooth. Add the reserved broth as needed. Salt to taste.

Once at the picnic, place a serving of hummus into the bottom of a jelly jar or clear plastic wine cup. Drizzle with olive oil, then poke fresh veggie spears of your choice into the dip and pass one to each picnicker.

Fire Roasted Eggplant Dip

1 large purple eggplant
2 cloves garlic, minced
2-3 Tbsp. tahini
Juice of ½ lemon
Salt to taste
Olive oil, optional smoked paprika and chopped parsley

At home, combine the garlic, lemon juice and tahini. Take to picnic in a small jar. At the campfire or grill, pierce the eggplants and place them on hot ash, turning often until blistered and soft. Remove skin and scoop hot pulp into a bowl along with the tahini, lemon and garlic. Blend well and season to suit you with salt and paprika. Drizzle with olive oil, sprinkle with parsley and serve out of the bowl with pita chips or crisp sweet red pepper wedges.

Spreads AND Dips

Photo by Henry Whittier Frees

Smoked Trout Dip Spread

Look for packages of smoked trout in the seafood section of your grocery or order it online from specialty shops. Or make your own, of course! Any type of smoked fish will do for this recipe as long as it's not "cold smoked." Slather trout spread on slices of dark rye bread topped with cucumber or serve with cut veggies for dipping. Colorful bell peppers, cucumbers and fresh dill adore smoked fish.

> 6-8 oz. smoked trout
> 4 oz. cream cheese or 4 Tbsp. sour cream or Greek yogurt
> 3 Tbsp. mayonnaise
> Zest and juice of ½ lemon
> 1 green onion, chopped fine
> 1 stalk celery, chopped fine
> 2 Tbsp. chopped raw sweet pepper, any color
> 1 Tbsp. chopped fresh chives or dill or both
> Smoked or sweet paprika to garnish
> Sweet pickle relish to taste (optional)
> 1 tsp. prepared horseradish (very optional)

Mix the cream cheese and mayonnaise and beat in 1 Tbsp. of the lemon juice and all the zest. Add the trout and non-optional ingredients and mix well. Now taste. Thin with remaining lemon juice if needed. Add optional ingredients to your liking. If you want this as a spread, keep it thick. Or thin with plain yogurt, cream or pickle juice for a dip.
Note: No smoked fish? Substitute 8 oz. canned salmon, drained

Spreads and Dips

Deviled Ham Spread

Yes, deviled ham.

The Underwood version of this curious, iconic spread has been around since 1868. If you were born before 1975, you've no doubt eaten it on family road trip picnics. In a white bread sandwich with pickles and potato chips, of course. By the way, it was an 1896 collaboration between Underwood's grandson and researchers at M.I.T. that created groundbreaking methods for safe high-temperature canning technology moving into the 20th century.

"Deviling" is nothing more than adding spices to a food. I like the creepiness of the early Underwood ham devil, who has evolved to a more playful fellow over the last century. Serve this savory spread on crackers, in a sandwich or as a deviled egg filling. Especially good on cucumber rounds and crunchy bell pepper strips, bundled in purple cabbage leaves and stuffed into celery gutters.

½ lb. ham, cut into cubes (I prefer an uncured, lower salt ham)
2 Tbsp. chopped onion
3-4 Tbsp. mayonnaise
1 Tbsp. your favorite mustard (or homemade, page 16)
1 tsp. Tabasco, Sriracha, or other hot sauce (to taste)
Non-official things you can add that create a chunky ham spread:
Parsley, chopped celery, sweet pickles, paprika

Combine ham, onion, mayonnaise and the mustard in bowl of a food processor. Blend until smooth-ish (how smooth is up to you). Add hot sauce to taste. A teaspoonful of sweet pickle relish or fresh lemon juice will cut the saltiness.

Ad from Printer's Ink Magazine, Sept. 11, 1907

Travel Bites

Savory Bacon, Cheddar, Chive Cake Salé

Also known as "gateau de voyages" (travel cake), this savory, rustic French picnic cake already has its boots on, ready to walk out the door. Perhaps to be enjoyed on a mossy creek bank with a bottle of simple red wine and a crunchy radish or two. And you. Make it your own by switching out the savory add-ins according to the season and what's hiding in your larder. It freezes well, sliced or whole.

1¼ cup all-purpose flour (can use up to ¾ cup cornmeal)
1 tsp. baking powder
¼ tsp. salt (up to ½ tsp. if not using salty bacon or sausage)
½ tsp. coarse cracked black pepper
3 eggs
½ cup buttermilk (or milk mixed with a spoonful of yogurt)
4 Tbsp. olive oil or melted butter
½ cup chopped cooked bacon (about 4-5 slices)
1 medium roasted pepper cut into ¼-inch pieces
4 oz. cheddar cheese, crumbled or grated
2 Tbsp. minced chives or ¼ cup chopped green onions
½ cup lightly toasted pecans, halved (optional)

Preheat oven to 350° and butter a 9-inch loaf pan. Mix flour, baking powder, salt and black pepper in one bowl and whisk together eggs, oil and buttermilk in another. Add wet to dry and stir until barely mixed. Gently fold in the remaining ingredients. Pour into prepared pan and bake for about 40 minutes until firm and browned. The cake travels well pre-sliced. It's also fabulous toasted.

Travel Bites

Cherry Apricot Oat Journey Bars

You won't believe how good these not-too-sweet bars taste when you're having a bit of a roadtrip food emergency. Store them wrapped individually in your freezer for grab-and-go adventures. I even take them on overseas trips as they keep well unrefrigerated for at least two weeks. This recipe makes 12 bars.

1 cup rolled oats
½ cup sliced toasted almonds
½ cup dried cherries or cranberries
2 Tbsp. brandy, other liqueur or fruit juice
½ cup dried apricots, roughly chopped
2 Tbsp. maple syrup or honey
1 Tbsp. coconut oil or melted butter
1 egg
½ cup mixed seeds ... pumpkin, sunflower, sesame, flax, etc.
2 Tbsp. oat flour or all-purpose flour
¼ tsp. salt
1 Tbsp. each of melted butter and maple syrup for brushing

Preheat oven to 350°. Warm the brandy, then add the cherries and allow them to soften while you prepare the other ingredients. Chop apricots finely in a food processor. Add cherries and their soaking liquid, maple syrup, coconut oil, and egg and pulse about 3 or 4 times. In a separate bowl, blend the oats, flour, seeds, salt and nuts. Add the dry ingredients to the wet and pulse a couple times. Press the mixture extra firmly with wet hands into a parchment paper-lined 7 x 11 inch (2-quart) glass baking dish. Mix the melted butter with the maple syrup and brush over all. Bake until golden brown, about 25 minutes. Keep uncut bars in baking dish and allow to cool completely before cutting into 12 bars.

Note: If you don't have a food processor, just finely mince the apricots with a knife. If the apricots are dry, blend them with an extra tablespoon of brandy or other liquid.

Crackers

omemade crackers are a picnic basket's best friend. Both lightweight and versatile, they are sure to delight your guests. Crackers freeze well, so make a big batch. Come picnic day, pack them in a vintage tin or individually wrap them in a twine-tied glassine or clear treat bag.

Oat crackers, cheese, berries and rosé wine

Hand-hewn Oat Crackers

An enduring favorite, I include these tender, rustic oat crackers in most of my gatherings and picnics. They never fail to delight guests when served with a bit of cheese and a dollop of homemade jam.

1 cup rolled oats
¾ cup all-purpose, unbleached flour
¼ tsp. baking soda
½ tsp. salt
1 Tbsp. brown sugar (optional)
5 Tbsp. cold unsalted butter, cubed
2 tsp. lemon juice
3-4 Tbsp. milk

Whirl dry ingredients in food processor just until mixed. Add butter and pulse a few times. Add a squirt of lemon juice and then 3 Tbsp. of the milk and pulse about ten times. Add the remaining milk until mixture is moist enough to clump but is not wet. Knead on a lightly floured board a couple times so it holds together enough to roll out. Place your dough on a piece of parchment paper that's the size of your 18 x 13 inch sheet pan. Cover dough with a piece of plastic wrap, then roll it out evenly about ⅛-inch thick. Remove plastic and cut with knife or pizza wheel into 1½-inch squares. Prick with fork. Slide dough-covered parchment onto sheet pan and bake at 375° about 12 minutes, until lightly browned. You may need to remove outer crackers as they brown, then continue to bake the rest until done.

Wheat-free version: Swap ¼ cup oat flour and ½ cup gluten-free flour blend for the all-purpose flour.

34

Crackers

Speedy, Seedy Wonton Wrapper Crackers

Sometimes you need a hurry-up cracker, not exactly made from scratch but, as we say around here, "Better than a poke in the face!"

—A good form of exercise.

Preheat oven to 350° and place wonton wrappers on a parchment paper-lined baking sheet (or buttered foil). Brush tops with beaten egg white mixed with a drizzle of toasted sesame oil (optional) and sprinkle with sesame seeds and a bit of coarse sea salt. Cut into 2-inch squares with a pizza wheel or knife and leave them where they lie. Bake until brown and crispy.

More toppings to try: grated Parmesan, chili flakes, finely minced rosemary.

Picnic tables made from ancient millstones, Taramundi, Spain

Crackers

Aunt Mary's Crunchy Cheese Crackers

Both my son, Wes, and my husband, Wayne, have requested these super crunchy treats for their last meal on earth. They think they're that good. Credit goes to my Aunt Mary of Athens, West Virginia, for tweaking this 1950s bridge party delight. If I were you, I'd hide them in the freezer from hungry fellers so you have enough to take to the picnic! Serve them in twine-tied clear treat bags.

8 oz. sharp cheddar cheese, grated
½ cup (1 stick) softened unsalted butter
1 cup all-purpose flour
1 tsp. baking powder
¼ tsp. salt
¼ tsp. cayenne pepper (to taste)
4 cups corn flakes, crush after measuring

Preheat oven to 350°. Sift flour, salt, baking powder and cayenne. Cream butter and grated cheese, then add the flour mixture. Beat just until combined. In a large bowl, measure out the cornflakes and crush them with the bottom of a glass into coarse crumbs. Add the cheese batter to the cornflakes and squish well with your hands. Form dough into one-inch balls and place them on a buttered or parchment paper-lined cookie sheet. Flatten the balls with the heel of your hand and bake about twelve minutes, or until golden brown and fragrant.

Note: To make gluten-free, use your favorite all-purpose flour blend and corn flakes that don't contain malt syrup.

Riverside breakfast picnic, Pembroke ,VA

Crackers

Crispy Orange Slice "Crackers"

Here's what people will say when you serve these crispy and super lightweight crackers at your next picnic gathering, "Do I eat the whole thing? Really? Oh my gosh, I can't believe these are so good!" They're not only great to munch on as a healthy snack, they're also fabulous on salads, and added to your tea, mulled cider or wine. Citrus and cheese aren't common bedfellows, but a log made from a fresh cheese like

chevre, fromage blanc or farmer's cheese mixed with dried cranberries (soaked in orange liqueur, of course), lemon zest and rolled in walnuts will go well with your orange crackers.

Because we have a daughter with a serious gluten intolerance, we keep wheat, rye, and barley products at bay in our home so that she can eat with us often. I prefer foods like these orange "crackers" that never had gluten in them to begin with rather than swapping out flour blends, hence you'll find lots of gluten and grain free alternatives in this little book.

To make: When oranges are in season, choose thin-skinned and mostly seedless varieties such as Clementine, Moro blood orange, Cara Cara or Satusuma tangerines. Slice as thinly as possible and dehydrate at 135° until completely dry. Stored in a wide-mouth quart jar, they'll keep well all through the spring and summer. A mix of varieties and sizes is extra exciting.

Dried orange slices with fresh homemade fromage blanc

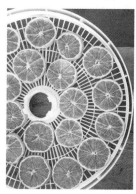

Dehydrating the oranges

Bread

Pepperoni Rolls

I f you're from West Virginia, as I am, you know that we're a tenacious bunch, stopping at nothing to defend all that we hold dear. Case in point: The pepperoni roll. Created in 1927 by Italian coal miner/baker, Giuseppe "Joseph" Argiro of Fairmont, these humble rolls spell home to natives of the north central region of the state.

Some 100 years ago, Italian laborers would purchase loaves of hearth-baked bread and sticks of cured meats for lunch en route to the mines each day. To simplify matters (and probably to keep coal dust off the miners' lunches), Argiro combined the two. He baked small loaves of bread with sticks of pepperoni-ish meats inside. Well, the guys loved it, he opened a bakery, and to this day, the rolls are prized by pretty much every north central West Virginian from every walk of life.

I grew up eating the pepperoni rolls from Tomaro's bakery in Clarksburg, so it's theirs that I yearn for. Soft inside and a bit crusty on the outside, the three sticks of pepperoni share a smear of orange-tinted grease with the innards of the rolls. They are shelf-stable and just the thing for a roadside picnic or ramble into the woods. Be forewarned, I have NO idea how Tomaro's bakery makes their rolls today (it's a carefully guarded secret), so I'm just recreating a rustic version based on childhood memories. My version calls for an overnight sponge that produces a flavorful roll which is definitely more crusty and chewy than the original, closer to a hearth-baked bread. But if I were you, I'd make a road trip pilgrimage to Clarksburg for the real deal!

Forming the rolls

The real Tomaro's small rolls which are semi-soft and light and mine which are crusty and enthusiastically stuffed with meat.

Bread

Rustic Italian Pepperoni Roll Dough

Italian bread is just flour, water, salt, yeast and sometimes a little olive oil. Adding the overnight sponge adds lots of flavor and texture to the dough, but it's not traditional. You can omit it, as long as you add the sponge ingredients to the rest of the dough. Once you knead your dough, you can refrigerate it up to a week until needed for rolls or pizza. If you're in a rush, any Italian bread recipe will work for the roll dough. For softer rolls, see variation below. Makes 10 smallish rolls.

The night before you bake, make your sponge by mixing:

½ cup water A pinch of instant yeast
1 scant cup (120 grams) of all-purpose flour

Cover, and in the morning, combine your bubbly sponge with:

½ cup water
1½ cups (195 grams) all-purpose flour
½ tsp. instant yeast
1 tsp. fine salt (¾ tsp. salt if adding lots of pepperoni)

Mix all ingredients well and let dough stand in the bowl 30 minutes, covered. The dough should be too wet to knead on a board. Just keep it in the bowl and fold it over itself until it starts to become smooth. Dip your hands lightly in water once or twice when they get sticky. Gather dough into a ball, coat well with olive oil, then place into a clean bowl. Cover with a plate and let rise until doubled, about 2 hours.

To make pepperoni rolls, you'll need about 4 oz. of stick pepperoni. Place the dough on a floured board and cut into 10 pieces. Form into balls, dust well with flour, and cover with a towel while you slice your

pepperoni into 30 skinny three-inch sticks. Gently stretch each dough ball into a square, lay out three meat sticks, roll up and pinch edges. Place on a buttered or parchment paper-lined sheet pan and let rise about 60 minutes, covered with a towel. Bake in a preheated 450° oven about 15 minutes until brown.

Soft Rolls: Keep the sponge as is. Add 1 Tbsp. olive oil or softened unsalted butter and 2 tsp. sugar to the remaining ingredients. Bake at 400° until nice and brown.

Bread

Effie's Buttermilk Skillet Cornbread

Effie Price was born in 1914 and raised in what is now our remote Appalachian log cabin. She and I broke many a hunk of black skillet cornbread together over the years, and I miss her terribly. Every time I make this bread, it's as though Effie's right there with me in my kitchen, so I make it often! Seek out fresh stoneground cornmeal and full-fat cultured buttermilk if you can. Individual servings made in antique cast iron gem pans (pictured right) or cornstick pans are especially handy for picnics. This recipe makes about 20 thin cornsticks or gems.

Snow picnic cornbread

2 cups stone-ground cornmeal (either yellow or white)
1 tsp. baking powder
¾ tsp. salt
¼ tsp. baking soda
1 egg
1⅓ cups buttermilk
5 Tbsp. melted unsalted butter + a bit to grease the skillet

Preheat oven to 425°. Place a 10-inch cast iron skillet or two cornstick pans in oven. Meanwhile, toss dry ingredients together in a bowl. In another bowl, whisk wet ingredients well. Add wet to dry and stir until just mixed. If your buttermilk is thick, you may need to add a tablespoon or two extra. Remove hot skillet from oven, add a small knob of butter and pour batter into pan. Bake about 25 minutes until golden brown (15 minutes in cornstick pans). Turn out of skillet at once so that the underside doesn't get soggy.

Effie hugs her mom on washin' day at our Madison County, NC, cabin, 1930s

Thermos Soups

For ease of serving in a primitive setting, pack creamy-ish textured soups in your thermos bottle. Otherwise, one person will get chunks and everyone else gets broth!

Corn on the Cob Soup

19th century cookbooks have plenty to teach us about discard-less cooking, not the least of which is corn cob broth. If you're not already acquainted with this marvelous method of adding flavor to your corn dishes, you're in for a treat. When corn is plentiful, I break in half and boil every single cob whose kernels have been stripped (prior to eating!) for at least 30 minutes in enough water to cover. After removing the cobs, I concentrate the broth by simmering a bit and then it goes into 8 oz. jelly jars to be frozen, then added to soups all winter. Sometimes I just stockpile naked cobs in the freezer, in plastic bags. A halved corncob or two gets tossed into veggie soups or any stew containing corn.

This corn on the cob soup can be served hot or cold, is delightfully uncomplicated and sings of summer.

> 1 ear of really good fresh corn per picnicker
> About 1 tsp. butter per ear of corn
> Salt and pepper to taste

Cut kernels from corn and then run the knife over the cob to remove the pulp. Set aside. Break the cobs in half, and add water just enough to cover. Simmer, lid on, for 30 minutes. Remove cobs and continue to simmer until you have about ½ cup of broth per person. Purée one cup of the corn broth along with the kernels and pulp in food processor or blender until it's as smooth as you like. Add more of the broth as needed until desired consistency. Back into the saucepan it goes on low heat. Add a little butter, lots of fresh ground pepper and salt to taste. This is a wonderful use for your seasoned garlic salt (page 17). Pour into thermos bottle and pack garnish separately. Maybe some croutons, a little fresh chopped dill, basil or paprika. Or nothing at all.

Thermos Soups

Cream of Celery Soup

—A bowl of good cream soup is a meal in itself.

Here's a cozy, creamy whole milk soup that pours beautifully from a vintage thermos bottle. My favorite soup for a snow picnic, it can be made with either corn, veggie or chicken stock. For a little added crunch, top with brown butter cornbread croutons (see facing page).

2 cups diced celery
1 cup diced celeriac (see note)
½ yellow onion
2 cloves garlic
1 Tbsp. butter

1 bay leaf
1 cup chicken stock
1 cup water
2 cups milk
1 Tbsp. cornstarch

Sauté celery, onion and garlic in butter until soft. Add 1 cup corn, vegetable or chicken stock plus celeriac and the bay leaf and simmer until soft. Remove bay leaf and run mixture through a food processor or blender with one additional cup water. Return to pot with 1 Tbsp. cornstarch dissolved in 1 cup of the milk. Barely simmer until thickened and add additional milk as needed. Season with fresh ground pepper and salt to taste. Heat but don't boil. If you want the soup to be greener, purée a leaf of kale or spinach along with your celery.

Note: Celeriac or celery root looks like a big, creepy, round, hairy root. Underneath that fearsome exterior lies a crunchy mild celery-scented tuber that's just wonderful in soups or with potato. You can swap a white potato for the celeriac if needed. For a vegetarian soup, use vegetable broth or corn cob stock (page 41).

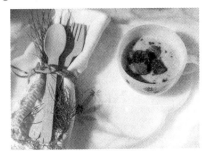

Snow picnickers enjoy cream of celery soup with cornbread croutons

Thermos Soups

Summer Gazpacho-ish Soup

A cool summer salad-y rendition of gazpacho that's as good as your tomatoes, so gather flavorful heirloom varieties if you can. If you prefer a puréed gazpacho, stick to a mono-color scheme of veggies. Carry to your picnic in a quart jar or thermos bottle. Serves 4-6

1½ lb. wonderful, juicy summer tomatoes, about 4 medium
2 small unpeeled thin-skinned cucumbers
½ small red onion, chopped
1 medium colorful bell pepper, chopped
1 clove garlic, smashed
2-4 Tbsp. sherry (or red wine) vinegar
2 Tbsp. good olive oil
½ jalapeno, minced or other hot pepper
¼ tsp. each salt and pepper, or to taste
½ tsp. paprika
A few thinly sliced basil or cilantro leaves

Gazpacho goes on a River picnic

Place quartered tomatoes in a blender and process until chunky. Add the remaining veggies, 2 Tbsp. of the vinegar and seasonings. Process until veggies are finely chopped but not liquefied. Adjust the seasonings, adding more vinegar to taste. Stir in cilantro or basil. Serve chilled.

Brown Butter Cornbread Croutons

Cut leftover cornbread into ½-inch cubes. Drizzle with brown butter (page 18) and spread evenly on a baking sheet. Bake at 325° until crunchy throughout. Season to taste with salt and fresh-ground pepper. Store/hide in freezer until picnic day.

Daughters Rita & Annie take me on a birthday picnic

Salad Dressings

nough already with the heavy mayo-based summer picnic salads! Well, almost. Save them for the big crowds and think vibrant and fresh for your more intimate warm-weather picnics. The now-popular rainbow varieties of carrots, beets, beans, onions and tomatoes that grace farm stands, groceries and home gardens make for spectacular salads that need only a simple vinaigrette to complete their ensemble.

Fresh Grated Apple Vinaigrette

½ apple, grated
2 Tbsp. walnut or olive oil
1 tsp. Dijon mustard

2 Tbsp. apple cider vinegar
1 Tbsp. minced shallot
1 tsp. honey

Purée vinegar, oil, mustard, shallot, and honey with a stick blender. Stir in grated apple and add salt and pepper to taste.

Use on: Carrot, cabbage, golden or striped beet salads. Also on kale salads or fall salads that contain walnuts. *Serves 4.*

Blackberry Vinaigrette

¼ cup blackberry pulp (squish a handful of berries)
¼ cup good olive oil
¼ cup balsamic vinegar
A sprinkle of salt and grinding of pepper

Use: Marinate raw matchstick-cut purple beets in vinaigrette and add to lettuce or pungent greens once at the picnic or eat as-is along with fresh blackberries and perhaps a lump of chèvre. *Serves 4.*

Herb Garden Buttermilk Dressing

1 cup good buttermilk
2 Tbsp. sour cream or Greek yogurt
1 clove garlic, smashed or big pinch herb garlic salt (page 17)
One handful mixed fresh tender herbs of your choice:
      chives, scallions, basil, parsley, tarragon, dill
Squirt of lemon juice
Salt and pepper to taste

Combine all ingredients and whirl in food processor or blender until mixture is a beautiful light green but herbs are still visible.

Use: As a veggie dip or drizzle on whole leaves of crunchy Bibb lettuce.

Salads AND Slaws

Creamy Slaw

Just in case you need to get your hands on a nice creamy slaw recipe, this one's pretty standard. Season to your tastes. Serves 6-8.

½ each of a small green and a red cabbage, thinly sliced
2 carrots, julienned or grated
1 green onion, thinly sliced
Slaw Dressing:
1½ cup mayonnaise (you can swap out Greek yogurt for part)
1 tsp. apple cider vinegar
1 tsp. Dijon (or your homemade) mustard
1 tsp. sweet pickle juice, cider syrup, or honey
Salt and pepper to taste
¼ tsp. celery seed (optional)
If you prefer crunchy slaw, pack prepared veggies and dressing separately and combine at the picnic.

Carrot Salad in Purple Cabbage Cups

A picnic salad made from just-plucked sweet carrots really needs nothing more than a squirt of fresh lemon juice. Golden raisins are fun, but they're totally optional. A julienne cut really maintains the carrot crunch if you have the gizmo to do it. As for the oil in this recipe, I prefer a nut oil like walnut or hazelnut but olive oil will do. Take the carrot salad to the picnic in one container and in a separate bag, a stack of red cabbage leaf-cups. This salad is gorgeous! Serves 4.

½ lb. good, fresh carrots, julienned or grated, any color
A sprig of parsley or cilantro, chopped
½ cup golden raisins or apples cut into matchsticks
3 Tbsp. grated apple vinaigrette (left) or juice of half a lemon
1 Tbsp. or so of oil (nut or olive)
Drizzle of honey if using lemon juice instead of vinaigrette
Salt and pepper to taste

Salads AND Slaws

Three Bean Salad in a Party Dress

I wish you could see this salad in color. It is truly is gorgeous. Visit your favorite farm stand in July and have fun selecting from popular vibrant veggie varieties. Serves 4-6.

½ lb. green beans
½ lb. yellow beans
1 small red onion, cut into thin strips
1 orange bell pepper, cut into thin strips
Handful halved cherry tomatoes
1½ cups cooked and drained garbanzo beans (or a 15 oz. can)

Boil beans a minute or two in salted water just until they turn a darker shade of green or yellow. Plunge into a bowl of cold water. Drain and mix with remaining ingredients and the vinaigrette. Top salad with brown butter cornbread croutons if you dare (page 43).

Vinaigrette: ¼ cup each apple cider vinegar and olive oil, one garlic clove smashed and minced, perhaps a drizzle of something sweet, and salt and pepper to taste.

Plum, Cucumber & Pickled Red Onion Salad

Crisp garden-fresh cucumbers mingled with tart/sweet plums make for uncommonly good salads that are both pretty and refreshing on a sweltering summer day. The fresher your produce, the better this salad.

Cucumbers	Rice wine vinegar
Plums	Cider syrup or honey
Red onion	A good pinch of salt

A specific recipe is not needed for this salad, especially because your summer produce will be so variable in size. For each serving, allow one cup of veggies. Thinly slice an equal volume of tart red plums and thin-skinned pickling cucumbers. Half as many red onions is about right, sliced in thin strips, tip to tail. Cover the onions in rice wine vinegar sweetened to your taste with a little drizzle of honey or apple cider syrup (see page 16), and a pinch of salt. Let onions marinate at least an hour. Pack onions and cuke/plum mixture separately into your cooler. Combine the two no more than an hour before serving.

Salads AND Slaws

Our Appalachian mountain cabin

Warm "Kilt" Spring Greens Salad

Get out your tin can stove and your boots, dears. We're heading into an Appalachian mountain holler for a little early springtime foraging. First stop, the abandoned apple orchard, where the prized morel mushrooms are poking up through the leaf litter here and there. Just down the hill, we spy a stunning patch of young and tender ramps (wild leeks). But my favorite fleeting woodland edible of all is growing atop moss-covered rocks in the icy cold creek. *Saxifraga micranthidifolia,* better known as branch lettuce, is the wild killed (wilted) salad green of your dreams.

I learned about "kilt" salads from my dear friend, Effie Price, who was born in what's now our remote and very rustic off-grid Madison County mountain cabin. *"In April, pick a mess of branch lettuce out of the creek before the plant begins to flower,"* she instructed. *"Then fry up a little piece of streaky meat (salt pork) or bacon. Wilt the branch lettuce with a little of the hot grease, add the meat and have it with a little piece of cornbread and some buttermilk. That's supper!"*

Make a killed green salad out of any sturdy green including kale, Bibb lettuce, watercress, arugula or creasy greens. Carry your greens to the picnic washed and torn, then drizzle with a little hot bacon grease. Add charred or pan-fried green onions or ramps, a sprinkle of cider vinegar, maybe a few flakes of hot pepper. Buttermilk cornsticks, yes!

Morels, ramps, nettles (above), branch lettuce (right)

47

Salads  Slaws

Cucumber and Melon Salad Skewers

Slice equal amounts of cucumbers, cantaloupe and watermelon into same-size chunks. Add a squirt of lime juice, a few mint leaves and a sprinkling of salt. Thread onto skewers and eat as-is or skip the salt and add to a glass of icy mint tea or chilled fizzy Portuguese Vinho Verde.

Crackly Brown Butter Quinoa Sprinkles

Even quinoa-haters will find the buttery crunch of this delightful superfood addictive. Take to your picnic and sprinkle on anything that needs a little pizzazz. Delightful on kale salads. Makes one quart which I recommend you hide from yourself in the freezer.

> 2 cups uncooked quinoa   1 tsp. salt
> 3 cups water   4 Tbsp. brown butter
> Optional spices: smoked paprika, cayenne, cumin, turmeric

Rinse the quinoa well in a colander. Boil water, add quinoa and ½ tsp. salt. Cover and simmer on low heat for 12-15 minutes, until tender. Dump onto a large baking sheet. Lightly stir in the butter and remaining ½ tsp. salt. Spread the quinoa over your baking sheet evenly and bake in a 325° oven for about 60 minutes, or until crispy, stirring every 20 minutes. Add any other spices you might like while warm. Allow quinoa to cool completely, then store in a quart jar in the freezer.

Maple brown butter version: Add 1 Tbsp. maple syrup along with the brown butter, and then half-way through baking, stir in another Tbsp. or two of syrup and a pinch of hot pepper. Keep an eye on the mixture as it browns quickly toward the end.

— Creaming the butter for the sandwiches. Notice how thin the slices of bread have been cut.

Sandwiches

andwiches really are a motor picnic's best friend. Speakin' of which, did you know that there were at least 450 automobile manufacturers in the United States prior to 1917? Relatively few of these companies have survived and the same goes for sandwiches. Just one look at the fabulous 1909 *Up-to-Date Sandwich Book,* and you'll be wondering why popcorn sandwiches lost favor. Maybe it was the anchovies and ketchup in the mix? I must say that I'm rather curious about this automobile sandwich:

Automobile Sandwich
Run through the meat chopper two pounds of cold boiled ham, half a pound of walnut meats, and four (small) dill pickles. Mix with a little French mustard, and place between slices of lightly buttered bread.

Any of the spreads included in this picnic book (or in your own repertoire) will make dandy sandwich innards, but it's also fun to head back 100 years or so for a bit of sandwich-makin' advice.

Let's talk bread. According to our *Up to Date Sandwich Book* ...

> "The first requisite in the preparation of good sandwiches is to have perfect bread in suitable condition. Either white, brown, rye, or entire wheat bread may be used."

And what is perfect bread, you might wonder?

> "New bread is best, but for inexpert cutters, loaves just one day old are the best. A close-made bread should be chosen, or thin sandwiches will be a failure." *Economical Cookery,* 1918.

Or, rather than choosing a bread that fits with your fillings, you can go around the back door and start with a great loaf of artisan bread and then let it determine the sandwich's destiny. So a dense loaf of German Vollkornbrot rye prefers to be sliced super thinly and bestowed with spreads rather than chunky fillings. Crusty French ficelle or slender Italian loaves are happy being sliced down the middle, filled with shaved ham, cheese, greens and tomato, then wrapped in parchment paper and tied with string. And, of course, don't discount the value of a loaf of store-bought sliced bread, a jar of peanut butter and another of jelly packed snugly into your backseat motor hamper.

Sandwiches

The Forgotten Art of Sandwich Making

About sandwich wrapping:

If it's been on your mind to cut down on plastic food wraps, then you need look no further than mid-20th century and earlier picnic books for inspiration such as this from 1918: "*Sandwiches for picnics should be wrapped in paraffin waxed paper to keep them moist or placed in a tin box lined with paper.*" If no paraffin paper was available, a damp napkin was wrapped around the sandwiches. Waxed paper beats the heck out of plastic wrap, if you ask me. Plus, you can save the spent paper to start a fire in your hobo stove. A peanut butter and plum jam sandwich lovingly wrapped in waxed paper and tied with twine (with a flower tucked in), turns an ordinary road trip into an adventure.

About butter smearage:

The only thing I didn't love about my grandmother Maudie's cooking was what she did to the ham sandwiches she made for our road trip back home. Between the slices of beloved, deliciously stinky salt rising bread went a thick slice of sweet-salty ham, a dab of mustard, Buttercrunch lettuce from her garden and a big old horrifying smear of butter. Born in 1892, she grew up in the era of "all sandwiches have butter." Period. Case closed. If Grandmother had made us these delicate floral-scented butter sandwiches from the 1909 *Up to Date Sandwich Book*, maybe I would have been a tad more accommodating.

VIOLET SANDWICH "Cover the butter with violets overnight. Slice white bread thinly and spread with the butter. Put slices together and cover with the petals of the violets."

ROSE-LEAF SANDWICH "Flavor fresh butter with the scent of rose by packing in a closed jar with a layer of rose petals and leaving several hours. Any fragrant rose will answer. Cut white bread into dainty strips or circles, spread with the perfumed butter, put one or two rose leaves between the slices, allowing the edges to show."

CLOVER SANDWICH "Trim the crust from a loaf of bread and place bread in a stone jar with clover blossoms. Wrap the butter in cheesecloth and also place in the jar. Leave overnight. Slice the bread thinly and spread with the clover-scented butter. Put two slices together and garnish with a clover blossom." *~Up to Date Sandwich Book, 1909*

Breadless Sandwiches

Not a bread eater? No problem, there are plenty of fun alternatives.

Pancetta bowl BLT

Pancetta bowl BLTs

Bake round Italian-style bacon slices on the backside of a muffin pan at 350°. Place a sheet pan underneath to catch the fat. If you can't find pancetta, lean strip bacon (not thick sliced) will work as well. You'll need to weave the strips to stabilize the bowl. Stack cooked bacon cups and fill at picnic with lettuce and a drizzle of mayonnaise. Top with thinly sliced tomato.

Crunchy Bibb lettuce cups

Cabbage leaves or baby bok choy stalk lined with a dollop of sandwich fillings will leave you feeling perky and refreshed on a hot summer day.

Poke sandwich ingredients onto bamboo skewers

Cheese, meat, cucumber, lettuce, olives, cherry tomatoes, pickles. If serving to kids, snip pointy end off after filling skewer.

Asian-style uncooked spring roll wraps

Make at home with moistened rice paper stuffed with all matter of garden veggies and fresh herbs. Serve with your favorite dips, including peanut sauce (recipe below). They do tend to stick together a bit, so you might want to wrap them individually in a bit of waxed paper or other wrap if tossing them into a picnic basket or backpack.

Cucumber rolls with peanut dipping sauce

Slice cucumber longways into thin strips with a sharp knife. Starting at one end, lay out a couple fresh basil leaves, then top with a little pile of matchstick-cut raw colorful garden veggies such as carrots, sugar snap peas, onion, pepper, yellow squash. Roll up and secure end with a toothpick. Serve at the picnic with peanut sauce for dipping.

Quick peanut sauce

6 Tbsp. peanut butter, 1 Tbsp. soy sauce, juice of a lime, 4 Tbsp. water, a grating of fresh ginger, pinch brown sugar and chili flakes. Give the mixture a whirl with an immersion blender or a short melt on stove top or microwave just to combine.

Veggies

ometime this summer, you might feel the calling to tote your tin can stove and wee frying pan out to the back yard just to celebrate the moment. Cold hoppy beer, hot and crunchy garden-fresh Parmesan-fried squash, a sky lit by lightning bugs and the good company of your nearest and dearest ... now that's a picnic I can agree with!

Do you See the Sweethearts in the Moon?

Parmesan-Fried Squash

Slice yellow squash (or zucchini if that's all you have) into rounds about ¼ inch thick. Quickly pan-fry in a tiny bit of butter on one side. Flip over when brown and place a thin slice of good Parmesan cheese on top of each round. When the bottom is browned, flip the squash, cheese side down. After one minute, turn off the heat. Wait another minute and then you can remove the squash from the pan. The cheese side should be nice and crunchy. Eat out of the pan, please.

Caramelized Carrots

The particulars don't really matter with this recipe. Once you make these seductive carrots, you'll get the idea. I keep a jar containing equal amounts of freshly milled coriander and cumin in my rocket stove picnic basket during carrot season.

Butter	Ground cumin and coriander
Honey	Lemon wedges

Whole carrots with ½ inch of stem attached, root hairs snipped

Cut large carrots in half, lengthwise. Keep smaller carrots whole. Place in a skillet with water to barely cover and add a drizzle of honey, a pat of butter and a sprinkle each of ground cumin and coriander. Simmer until liquid evaporates, shaking the pan as you go. Brown carrots to your liking. Add a squirt of lemon juice, and season with salt and pepper.

Hobo rocket stove fired up and ready for carrot cooking

Veggies

Campfire or Iron Pot Corn on the Cob

Pull corn husk back to remove silk. Replace the husk and soak the corn in water so that the husk is good and wet. If going on a day cookout, prep at home and transport the damp corn in a waterproof bag. Grill over embers about 15 minutes, turning when necessary. Or you can throw the corn in a Dutch oven with lid on, and set the pot on embers, turning corn as it browns. Serve with a little salted butter, brown butter or any of the flavored butters below.

Husking Corn for the Picnic, 1896
Photo Courtesy Library of Congress

Herb Butter Flavors for Corn on the Cob
See page 19 for more information on how to make herb butters.

⇒ Cilantro, red onion, jalapeno pepper, lime zest, salt and pepper
⇒ Chive, finely grated Parmesan cheese, salt and pepper
⇒ Chopped fresh dill, minced chili pepper, salt and pepper
⇒ Blend basil, salt and pepper in a food processor with softened butter until the spread is a beautiful light green color.

Dutch Oven Baked Potatoes

Oil and lightly salt fresh fingerling potatoes. Put them in a Dutch oven with coals on top and underneath. Bake until brown and crispy, about 30-40 minutes. Great use for your garlic salt.

Old friends catch up while roasting corn, eggplants and peaches in the backyard campfire.

Pickles

See this poor feller here? That's what's going to happen to you if you don't include pickles in each and every one of your picnic outings! Okay, maybe that's a bit dramatic, but the crunch and acidity offered by a homemade pickle will most definitely liven up all your portable meals.

Interesting store-bought pickles are readily available at specialty markets, but why not make your own? Hurry-up refrigerator/cooler pickles will be ready to enjoy an hour after you assemble the ingredients and you'll love adding your own bread and butter pickles to picnic salads and deviled eggs. Just about any vegetable can be pickled with minimal equipment either by brining with salt or by marinating the veggies in a variety of vinegars. If you're interested in canning vinegar or brined pickles, contact your local county extension office for safe canning guidelines.

I'M IN AN AWFUL
PICKLE

A Few Pickling Tips

⇛ For crunchy pickles, slice blossom end off cucumbers to remove the enzyme which will make them soft.

⇛ Use non-chlorinated, filtered water.

⇛ Make your pickles out of the very freshest produce. Perky cell walls = happy pickles.

⇛ Experiment with your favorite vinegars. Combine an excellent apple cider vinegar with cider syrup for sweetening.

⇛ Pickling salt is very fine grained, dissolves easily and has no anti-caking agents. You can swap 2 Tbsp. Diamond Crystal kosher salt for 1 Tbsp. pickling salt. Other brands of kosher salt contain anti-caking ingredients and measure differently by weight. Sea salts often contain minerals that can discolor pickles.

⇛ The following recipes are for unsealed refrigerator pickles which will last a month or more in your fridge. To can for shelf-stability, you'll need to consult a recipe specific to that purpose.

Pickles

Refrigerator Dill Pickles

2 lbs. little Kirby pickling cucumbers
6 heads fresh dill flowers or 2 tsp. dill seeds
½ tsp. each mustard seed & peppercorns
2 small dried chili peppers, whole
4 cloves garlic, peeled
4 tsp. pickling salt
1½ cups white distilled or cider vinegar
2 cups filtered water

Pack a ½ gallon jar or 2 quart jars with whole, fresh-picked, tender cukes (blossom ends removed). Layer with the dill heads, seeds, peppers and garlic. In a saucepan, bring vinegar, water and salt to a boil and pour over the pickles. Cool and refrigerate. Let them sit a couple of days before eating. They'll last about a month.

Hurry-Up Ice Box Pickles

So-called "hurry-up" recipes were all the rage in late 19th century cookbooks. Many delightfully irreverent instruction books were penned by women for fellow exhausted housewives who cooked for their families and ran their homes without hired help. "Quick Cooking" by Flora Loughead, published in 1887, especially cracks me up. I'm pretty sure she would have approved of this ice box pickle recipe.

Slice an equal amount of fresh thin-skinned cucumbers and onion. Place in a shallow glass dish with lid. Cover with rice wine vinegar, a drizzle of honey to taste, a pinch of hot pepper and salt to taste. Chill.

Hurry-Up Pickled Red Onions

¾ cups white wine vinegar   ½ tsp. salt
1 Tbsp. sugar (or to taste)   1 red onion, thinly sliced
Optional ingredients: a few peppercorns, a smashed green cardamom pod or 3 allspice berries, definitely a small dried chili pepper

Bring vinegar, salt and sugar to boil. Cool a few minutes and combine with onions. Let sit for at least an hour. Will keep a couple weeks, refrigerated. Swapping out apple cider vinegar and 2 Tbsp. cider syrup or honey for the sugar makes tasty pickles, but they won't be as vibrant.

Pickles

Banana Pepper Rings

Use a variety of pepper colors and remove seeds if you prefer a milder pepper (use gloves). This recipe makes 2 pints.

> 1 lb. (about 12) banana peppers, cut into rings
> 2 cups cider vinegar   2 tsp. sugar
> 1 cup water   2 tsp. pickling salt

Bring the vinegar, water, sugar and salt to a simmer. Meanwhile, pack peppers into jars. Pour hot vinegar mixture over the peppers, topping off with a little water if needed. Cover and refrigerate.

Bread and Butter Pickle Chips

So easy to make when little thin-skinned pickling cukes are bountiful. This recipe makes a quart of crunchy pickles that are less sweet than is typical. Feel free to tweak according to your sweet or salty tastes.

> 1 lb. pickling cucumbers   1 tiny chili pepper (optional)
> 1 medium onion   2 tsp. mustard seeds
> 1 scant Tbsp. pickling salt ¼ tsp. celery seeds
> 1 cup cider vinegar   Few peppercorns
> ½ cup sugar   Big pinch turmeric

Choose super fresh, small Kirby pickling cucumbers and remove blossom ends. Slice them ¼-inch thick and place in a bowl along with thinly sliced onions. Add the salt and cover with ice cubes and about ¼ cup water. After 2 hours, drain mixture and rinse well. Pack veggies into

a quart jar. Meanwhile, bring remaining ingredients to a simmer and, once sugar dissolves, pour over cucumber mixture. Add a little water to cover pickles if needed. Cover and refrigerate.

Note: See page 54 for information on salt swapping.

Meat

ince it seems that nobody can resist poking a campfire, let's just go ahead and have a *skewered and poked* themed campfire picnic where each guest is included in the fiery fun. Invite your friends to bring a plate of raw, skewered and marinated veggies and/or meat to share as well as a pair of tongs. You provide the embers, a grill top or two propped up on bricks or logs, and platters for serving. Guests help with the cooking if they like and the skewers are shared as they come off the fire rather than all at once. Have some appetizers, beverages and a big bowl of picnic salad on hand along with a sliced watermelon, and you're set until marshmallow-cooking time.

Herb-Skewered Lemon Rosemary Meatballs

1 lb. ground turkey
1 lb. ground pork
1 cup total chopped red onion and colorful bell pepper
2 Tbsp. parsley and 1 Tbsp. fresh rosemary, minced
1 tsp. kosher salt and ½ tsp. black pepper
2 cloves garlic, minced
1 tsp. lemon zest
½ tsp. chili flakes (to taste)

Mix all ingredients well and form into 1½-inch balls. Place on a sheet pan and freeze. Pop frozen meatballs in a zipper bag and pull out what you need for each outing. They'll thaw by the time you get to your picnic. The easiest way to cook these over a live fire is to fry them up in an iron skillet over embers. When brown, add a big squirt of fresh lemon juice and a drizzle of white wine or water to the pan. Swirl the meatballs around in the sauce, and serve straight out of pan with skewers made of bamboo or woody-stemmed rosemary or lemon verbena. Or toothpicks, or even twigs. *Makes 80 bite-sized meatballs.*

Meat

Meat or Hashbrown Stuffed Campfire Onions

You can prep these stuffed onion halves at home and take them to the campfire wrapped up, ready to throw on hot embers. Chop up the onion you removed from the inside and add it to your stuffing mix.

Meatloaf or Lean Sausage Stuffing:
Cut medium unpeeled onions in half longways (from tip to tail). Remove a couple of the inside layers of onion, chop finely and add to a dab of sausage or meatball mixture. Rub onion halves with a little oil and add just enough meat to fill the onion cavity without mounding. Wrap with a little parchment paper followed by tightly-wrapped foil. Place adjacent to fire or on a thin bed of embers and cook about 10 minutes on each side or until they smell caramelized.

Photo courtesy Library of Congress

Vegetarian Hash Brown Stuffing:
Bake a waxy potato and refrigerate until cold. Grate with large holes of a box grater. Toss with a little melted butter and sprinkle with garlic herb salt (page 17) or seasoning of your choice. Pack into onion halves and bake as above.

Speedy Parmesan Baked Chicken

When fried chicken's not happening, this easygoing chicken can be thrown together quickly. It packs well, kids love it, and it's just dandy.

> Halved boneless chicken thighs and/or boneless breast strips
> About 2 Tbsp. melted butter per pound of chicken
> Panko bread crumbs
> Grated Parmesan cheese
> Spice possibilities: thyme, paprika, garlic herb salt, pepper

Melt butter in a glass baking dish big enough to hold your chicken. Rub chicken with butter, then dip in the bread crumbs that have been combined with the cheese and spices. Bake in a 375° oven about 30 minutes, or until cooked through and browned.

Meat

Forgotten Cider Pork

Forgotten foods are my specialty! On more than one occasion, I have slid the prepared pork into the iron pot, placed it in the oven or fireplace and forgotten about it for hours while attending to other chores at hand. The caramelized, flavorful meat is such a hit with diners, that now it's the first thing to go on the fire as the rest of the meal is being considered.

A picnicker sneaks a taste of pork

3 lbs. pork shoulder
4 cups apple cider (part hard cider is fun)
1 onion, cut into large pieces
Glug of Calvados (apple brandy), if you have it
1 tsp. fine salt (or about 1½ tsp. kosher), less is fine
Fresh ground pepper

Cut meat into 3-inch chunks. I remove the large pieces of fat (to render into lard later), but you use your own judgement. Rub salt and pepper into the meat and place in a bag along with the onion for

transport to your campfire. Prepare your Dutch oven by placing a few hot coals on top and underneath. Add the meat, onions, cider and Calvados, if using. Keep the temperature at about 300° or just under a simmer and when you remember, from one to four hours later, check on it. Serve the meat straight out of the pot.

Putting up apples in a make-do outside woodstove.

Photo courtesy of Mars Hill University

Not Meat

Summer Garden Veggie Burgers

Homemade veggie burgers can be a bit tricky to transport. It helps to chill separately wrapped burgers before you leave home. You can swap out other summer veggies, but just keep total amount to one cup.

1½ cups cooked and drained salted chickpeas (one 15 oz. can)
1 small zucchini, grated, liquid removed (see note below)
1 medium carrot, grated
1 green onion, chopped fine
Few sprigs parsley or cilantro, chopped
2 cloves garlic, smashed
1 egg
½ cup old fashioned oats
¼ cup toasted sunflower or pumpkin seeds
2 Tbsp. tahini (or other nut butter)
2 tsp. red wine (or other) vinegar
¼ tsp. each ground cumin and coriander
¼ tsp. each salt and pepper and optional hot pepper flakes

Put seeds and oats in food processor and rough chop. Add chickpeas and pulse a few times. Combine all other ingredients in a bowl, smush in the chickpea mixture and adjust the seasonings to suit you. Using a ⅓ cup measure, form into 8 patties, wrap individually, and grill or pan-fry at the picnic. They also freeze well. If cooking at home, let the patties sit at least 30 minutes before pan-frying in a little butter.
Note: Lightly salt grated zucchini while prepping other ingredients. Rinse well, place into cheesecloth and squeeze hard to remove liquid.

Fondue cheese mixture is first cooked in a vintage yard sale Revere Ware pan, then transferred to a 1970s era bright orange enamel fondue pot with a canned alcohol flame. A tin can rocket stove is great for this purpose but any portable burner will work just as well.

Not Meat

Tin Can Hobo Stove Cheese Fondue

It's the most fun picnic adventure ever! When making fondue on a portable stove, it's best to make small batches. If you don't have Kirsch (cherry brandy), swap other brandy or liqueur. Serves 2-4.

½ pound Gruyere cheese, grated   ½ cup dry white wine
1 Tbsp. cornstarch   2 tsp. lemon juice
1 garlic clove, peeled   1 Tbsp. Kirsch
Good pinch each of dry mustard, pepper and nutmeg
Dippers: pre-cut veggies, bread, bite-sized fruits

Coat the grated cheese with cornstarch and place in a plastic bag. Combine wine with lemon juice and place in a small jar. Bring the remainder of the bottle with you to drink. You may need a little extra Kirsch to thin the mixture, so plan accordingly when you pack. Once you're at your picnic location, assemble all your dippers and fondue sticks. Fire up your portable stove and rub the inside of your pan with the garlic clove. Add the wine and lemon juice to the pan and heat until simmering. Add cheese by small handfuls, stirring until blended before adding more. Keep stirring, taking the pan off the heat as needed to keep from boiling. After a few moments, the mixture will magically become creamy. Add the cherry brandy and then the pepper and nutmeg.

Hard Cider Fondue: Replace white wine with hard cider and swap apple brandy (Calvados is wonderful) for the Kirsch.

Brown Ale Fondue: Replace half the Gruyere with grated cheddar and either omit brandy or add whiskey for a boilermaker fondue.

Friends gather for a fondue party at an Asheville brewery

61

Bean Hole Beans

Beans. They are the finest product of the home brew. They are the richest noun in the dictionary. Bean-bag Magazine, 1921

Your life is about to change, thanks to the Native Americans of Maine who generously shared their earth buried bean baking secrets with European settlers back in the 1600s. Also known as "lumberman's beans," these hearty earth-baked legumes became a mainstay of the region's long-standing timber industry workers as well. If you haven't been to a New England Saturday night bean supper picnic, you'll want to start your own backyard bean-baking tradition with your friends and family.

First, we need some beans. Not any bean, mind you. We need heirloom Maine Yellow-eye, Jacob's Cattle, European Soldier or Marfax beans (see resources, page 77). These creamy beans hold their shape during the long, slow bake and they're well worth seeking out. Unlike many historic recipes, this one has evolved very little since the 1800s.

Dig the bean hole: If it's a permanent fixture in your backyard, dig it three feet wide and the same deep. Line the sides with flat rocks or bricks that fit well together. For a more temporary situation, dig the hole about a foot wider and 6 inches deeper than your bean pot.

Prepare the fire: Traditionally, the beans are baked in the pit overnight, but we're aiming for an evening party, so you'll be getting up early. About 4 hours before you're ready to bake, build a fire in your pit out of hardwood. When your pit is about ¾ full of embers, it's time to lay in the beans (see facing page for bean recipe). Shovel all but 2 inches of embers out of the bean hole into a metal wheelbarrow, or just onto the ground. Lower the pot of hot beans into the hole; be sure the handle is sticking up. Cover sides and top with embers and dry dirt. Place a piece of sheet metal on top, weighted with rocks. Or just mound dirt on top. After about 5-8 hours, invite your guests to help you dig up the beans.

Picnickers gather for bean hole pot pulling

Bean Hole Beans

Bean-hole Bean Recipe

2 lbs. heirloom beans (2 lbs. beans serves 8)
½ cup molasses (part maple syrup is nice)
2 tsp. dry mustard
1 onion, sliced
½ lb. salt pork cut into 2 x ½ inch cubes, fat scored

A note about salt: Cook a little piece of your pork in a pan, if it's really salty, omit salt from beans. Otherwise add 1 tsp. salt (to taste) to beans before baking in pit and adjust as they come out. I use uncured slab bacon instead of super-salty packaged salt pork, even though smoked meat is not quite traditional. The beans are also excellent without meat.

Prepare the beans: The night before your picnic, soak beans. Next morning, rinse well, cover with a couple inches of water and "parboil until the skins crack when you blow on them," about an hour. Pour beans and broth into a 6-quart Dutch oven with a tight-fitting lid. Add remaining ingredients, laying the salt pork on top of the beans. Add hot water, if needed, to cover beans by one inch (more if you like brothy beans). Place lid on and cover top securely with aluminum foil so ashes and dirt don't leak through during the bake. Bake in the bean hole from 5 hours to overnight, depending on your schedule.

Photos by Annie Erbsen

Oven Baked Bean-hole Beans

No time to dig a bean hole? Not to worry, these delightful heirloom bean hole beans from Maine bake up just fine in your home oven, preferably in a cast iron pot. Bake in a slow 275° oven with the lid on for 3-4 hours. Keep an eye on the liquid level and don't allow the beans to bake dry. Uncover toward the end and crank up the heat for a few minutes to get a little authentic char on the beans.

Desserts

hen it comes to portable picnic desserts, go with the season, keep it simple, and choose individual versions of your favorite confections. Hand pies, slice-and-bake icebox cookies, traybakes and sturdy pound cake slices are all good choices. But nothing beats fresh-picked summer berries and stone fruits eaten as-is or with a crunchy homemade cookie. Up first, however, is made-from-scratch s'mores – you'll need them for a campfire picnic.

Honey Graham Crackers

Graham flour is a coarsely milled 100% wheat flour containing the bran and germ. Sylvester Graham would roll over in his grave if he knew we were adding sugar to his beloved 1830s unsweetened health food namesake, let alone a square of chocolate and a toasted marshmallow!

1¼ cup all-purpose flour
1¼ cup graham flour (or 100% whole wheat)
1 tsp. baking powder
½ tsp. baking soda
½ tsp. salt
½ cup unsalted butter, softened
¼ cup brown sugar
3 Tbsp. honey
1 Tbsp. molasses (can swap honey)
3 Tbsp. cream or whole milk
1 tsp. vanilla and ½ tsp. cinnamon

Beat butter, sugar, honey and molasses until well blended. Mix in vanilla and milk. In a separate bowl, mix dry ingredients. Combine wet with dry and mix just until blended. Form dough into a ball that you can gently knead a few times. If too dry, add a bit more milk. Refrigerate for 30 minutes. Roll out thin as you can onto a parchment-lined baking sheet. Cut with a pastry or pizza wheel into the size you like and prick with a fork. You can also form into a log, chill and slice thinly. Bake at 350° for about 12 minutes until lightly browned.

Desserts

Summer Berry Marshmallows

Our backyard is morphing into a black raspberry bramble and we couldn't be happier. They sneak into about everything we eat for three weeks in June, including marshmallows (dipped in chocolate and frozen). You can use any summer berry to flavor

marshmallows. The berry adaptation follows the recipe for the vanilla version. You'll need a candy thermometer and stand mixer or powerful hand mixer for this adventure.

> 3 Tbsp. unflavored gelatin (3 packages)
> 1½ cups sugar
> 1 cup light corn syrup
> 2 tsp. vanilla extract
>
> 1 cup cold water
> Pinch salt

Butter (or spray with neutral oil) a 7 x 11 inch glass baking dish. Coat with a thin layer of sifted confectioners sugar. Into a large mixing bowl, stir together the gelatin and ½ cup of the cold water. Place the remaining ½ cup water, sugar, corn syrup and salt in a heavy pan over medium heat, and stir until sugar dissolves. When mixture boils, cover the pan with lid for 3 minutes to remove any crystals that form. Cook, uncovered (without stirring) until syrup reaches 240°F. Remove pan from heat and slowly pour over the gelatin in a thin stream, while beating on low until all syrup is added. Then beat at high speed about 12 minutes until very thick. You'll know it's done when it starts to get a little stringy and thick. If using a hand beater, the mixture will start to crawl up the beaters. Beat in the vanilla and pour the thick blob of marshmallow cream into the baking dish and smooth. Let sit overnight, uncovered. Remove from pan, cut with scissors or sharp knife and dust with powdered sugar. Keep in an air-tight tin or freeze.

Berry Mallows: Warm ¾ cup fresh or thawed berries and squeeze through a sieve to remove seeds. This juice/pulp will replace the ½ cup water that you mix with the gelatin. Add enough water to the juice to bring to ½ cup. If juice is thick with pulp, add an extra Tbsp. of water. Making s'mores? Berry mallows appreciate good bittersweet chocolate.

Desserts

Key Lime Curd, Yogurt and Berry Parfait

Carry ingredients separately to picnic and assemble right before eating. Into clear plastic wine glasses or glass jars, add a spoonful of plain (or vanilla) Greek yogurt, one of lime curd and a few berries. Continue layering, ending with berries. Garnish with a mint leaf, edible flower or lime wedge.

Key Lime Curd

This is a fairly tart curd. You may increase the sugar to suit your taste. Tangy Key limes are preferred, but common Persian limes will do. Citrus curds also make lovely tart fillings. Take mini prebaked tart shells to picnic and drop a dollop of lime curd into each. A tiny lime slice makes a fetching garnish.

> Juice and zest of one lemon
> Lime juice to make ½ cup when added to the lemon juice
> 1 tsp. lime zest (careful ... only the green part, the white is bitter)
> ½ cup sugar (up to ¾ cup)
> 2 whole eggs
> 6 Tbsp. unsalted butter, sliced
> Pinch salt (omit if using salted butter)

Juice the lemon and limes and set aside the zest. In a double boiler pan or metal bowl, whisk together the egg and the sugar. Add the juice and butter. We'll add the zest later. Place the bowl over simmering water and whisk for about 10-15 minutes until thickened. A dribble of the mixture should leave a trail on the top when done. Strain through a mesh sieve to remove any egg solids. Now, add the zest. Makes about 1½ cups of curd. Store in the refrigerator up to two weeks.

Pie pops and tiny tarts are fun picnic desserts

Fresh berry parfaits

Desserts

Caramel Oat Flapjacks Cookies

Known as a "traybake" in the British Isles, these super crunchy flourless oat cookies are my favorite hurry-up dessert. I haven't met a soul that can resist them after the first bite. Anything you bake in a "tray" is fine fodder for picnics.

> 7 Tbsp. butter
> 3 Tbsp. golden syrup, light corn syrup or brown rice syrup
> Scant ½ cup granulated sugar (not brown sugar)
> Pinch salt
> 2 cups rolled oats
> 1-2 Tbsp. sesame seeds (optional)

Tinkering options: Substitute sliced almonds, coconut, pumpkin seeds, etc. for up to ½ cup of the oats.

Preheat oven to 350° and lay a piece of parchment paper onto a 9x13 inch rimmed baking tray. In a saucepan, melt butter then add the syrup and sugar. Barely stir in oats and other seeds or nuts and salt just until blended. Spread the mixture onto the parchment paper evenly and bake until the mixture is bubbly and dark caramel in color. Start checking at 12 minutes. Remove the parchment along with hot flapjacks from pan to a board and let them set up a few minutes before cutting into small squares while still warm. Let cool completely before packing into a decorative tin.

Desserts

Bangor Brownies

Brownies were a fairly new invention when May Southworth suggested them as a good motor picnic dessert in her fantastic 1923 Motorist's Luncheon Book. *These fudgy style brownies are the real deal and they hold together well for rambling. I've included a slightly adapted version for you below.*

"Cream one half cup of butter with one cup of sugar. Add three squares of melted chocolate, two eggs, slightly beaten, one cup of chopped walnuts and one half cup of sifted flour. Bake in a moderate oven. Cut in oblong strips before removing from the tin."

½ cup unsalted butter   ½ tsp. salt
1 cup sugar   ½ cup flour
1 tsp. vanilla   2 eggs
3 oz. chopped bittersweet chocolate
1 cup lightly toasted walnut halves, rough chopped
Optional 2 Tbsp. cocoa powder for extra chocolaty-ness

Melt butter, then add chopped chocolate. Stir until chocolate melts. Whisk in sugar and vanilla. Mix in eggs, one at a time, and salt. Mix cocoa, if using, with flour and nuts. Add dry ingredients to wet and combine just until blended. Pour batter into a buttered 8x8 inch baking pan (lined with buttered parchment for easy removal), and bake in 350° oven for 20-25 minutes.

Almond Macaroon Bites

A simple, last minute happy cookie. Chewy and not too sweet.

2 cups almond meal   2 egg whites (don't whip)
½ cup sugar   ¼ tsp. almond extract
A good pinch salt

Combine almond meal, salt and sugar. Stir in egg whites and almond extract until well blended. Form into about three dozen 1-inch balls with your hands or use a 1-inch cookie scoop. Bake in a 300° oven for 30 minutes or until lightly browned.

Desserts

Slice-and-Bake
Shortbread Cookies

"When strawberries are in season, try serving them with real Scotch shortbread," instructs Good Housekeeping Magazine, *in June of 1908. As I write this, it's 16°F outside our mountain cabin door. The fantasy of a spring picnic, gingham blanket spread among the violets, warm sun, fresh plucked crimson strawberries with the crisp crunch of a lemon cornmeal shortbread cookie sounds pretty good right now! Pack these delicate cookies in a small tin or pasteboard box.*

Pack shortbreads in a tea tin

1 cup unsalted butter, room temperature
½ cup granulated sugar or ⅔ cup powdered sugar
2¼ cups all-purpose flour
¼ tsp. salt (crunchy salt is extra fun to bite into)
1 tsp. vanilla

Beat butter, sugar and vanilla until well blended. Combine salt and flour and then add to butter mixture. Beat a minute, just until dough comes together. Form into two logs, about the size of a paper towel tube, wrap and refrigerate or freeze. When ready to bake, slice a little shy of ½ inch, prick twice with a fork and bake at 325° about 15-18 minutes until very lightly browned.

Note: I much prefer granulated sugar over powdered. To keep it from being too grainy, "superfine" your raw or white sugar by whirling it in the food processor or blender a few minutes.

Brown butter/pecan: Use all or part brown butter, and add ½ cup ground pecans. Instead of white sugar, use brown.
Rosemary/lemon/cornmeal: Add 2 tsp. finely chopped rosemary and zest of a lemon. Swap ¼ cup cornmeal for same amount of flour.
Chocolate: Add 4 Tbsp. cocoa powder.
Maple Buckwheat: Swap up to 1 cup buckwheat for flour, use maple sugar in place of white and add ½ cup lightly toasted walnut pieces.

Box Lunch

My family moved from rural West Virginia to bustling Richmond, Virginia, when I was in my teen years. A beguiling southern city, Richmond is known for its grand architecture, gorgeous spring gardens, Civil War history and the home of Patrick Henry's 1775 *"Give me Liberty or give me death!"* speech. But if you ask me, "What's the heart and soul experience of the city that you don't want to miss?" I'll say, "It's a carry-out box lunch from Sally Bell's Kitchen."

Smack dab in the middle of downtown Richmond, Sally Bell's Kitchen has occupied the same charming brick building since 1942. While the third generation family-owned business has been serving up made-from-scratch fare since 1924 (originally across the street), they've been box-lunching it since the 1950s. And little has changed since then. It's like walking into a homey grandmother's kitchen time capsule where five of

the best southern picnic classics of your choosing are waiting to go into your pasteboard box, lined with waxed paper and tied up with a string. As if that's not enough, you're served/guided by capable and engaging ladies, many who have been a part of the Sally Bell's Kitchen family for decades.

The Sally Bell's Box Lunches Include:

Choice of sandwich (soft rolls with chicken salad, pimento cheese, cream cheese and olive, etc.)
Cup of potato or macaroni salad (with homemade mayo of course)
½ deviled egg (wrapped expertly in waxed paper)
A cheese wafer with pecan pressed into the top
Cupcake (iced upside-down to stay moist, so many flavors)

Box Lunch

A Sally Bell's customer picks up her box lunches at the beautiful blue counter

Box Lunch Goes on a Picnic With Friends

You can purchase paper take-out boxes, but upcycled shoe or small boxes are fun, especially if your kids decorate them with pages of old schoolwork or drawings that need a home. Line the inside of the box with waxed paper and, to cut down on additional packaging, include picnic foods that are their own wrappers. A bundle of veggie sticks tied with a green scallion strip or lettuce rolls filled with marinated potato salad and secured with a tooth-pick are a nice surprise. Toss in a few Aunt Mary's crunchy cheese crackers, a Bangor brownie, and fasten the box with a piece of twine.

Coney Island Picnic, NY, 1905
Photo Library of Congress

Campfire

You'll find recipes for a few campfire foods in the meat and the veggie sections of this book. But, really, you can cook anything on a campfire if you know a few basic techniques. My best ideas have hailed from the books penned by two of my favorite social reformers of yesteryear: Horace Kephart (*Camping and Woodcraft*, 1906) and Daniel Carter Beard (*American Boys Handy Book*, 1882). "It is quite impossible to prepare a good meal over a higgledy-piggledy heap of smoking chunks, a fierce blaze, or a great bed of coals that will warp iron and melt everything else," says Kephart. So let's talk fires.

Hunter-Trapper Fire

The Turkey Lay

My fire preference is somewhere between the "hunter-trapper" and the "turkey lay." Basically, I start with two logs, placed parallel about a foot apart. Tinder is placed between and then larger wood lays crossways on top. The glowing embers drop down between the logs, and can be easily shoveled out. Use them for grilling, a hobo fire between rocks or Dutch oven baking.

Corn bakes atop a grill placed on a *Turkey Lay* fire. Eggplants roast straight on live embers that have been shoveled out between the logs, and peaches are pan-grilled in a cast iron skillet over coals. When the corn comes off the fire, wood will be added to liven the flames while picnickers enjoy the meal. The fresh embers will be ready just in time for marshmallow roasting.

Campfire

A Few Suggestions for Campfire Picnics

Stick Baking: The Italian bread dough (page 39) works well for forming into "snakes" that you can wrap around a pointed roasting stick. Cook slowly over embers. How about stick-grilled fruits like pineapple, banana or peach dipped in a pot of warm spiced rum? Use sticks of green hardwood (no shrubs) and harvest responsibly.

Ember baking: Place whole beets, potatoes, onions, eggplants, etc. on slightly glowing embers. Turn with tongs as needed.

Foil baking: Line heavy duty foil with parchment paper. Fill packages and fold edges over several times to seal. Place on slow embers or at periphery of fire. Fish with herbs, lemon and onion is delicious baked this way, as are sweet or white potatoes, asparagus, stuffed peppers, peach halves, pretty much anything that can handle a bit of steam roasting along with the caramelization.

Grilling or skillet cooking: Place a portable grill or skillet atop a couple of small logs with embers below.

Leaf baking: Wrap ground meat or veggies in cabbage, collard or chard leaves and bury in coals.

Hot stone cooking: Bake thinly sliced and seasoned root veggies or zucchini on a hot stone.

Dutch oven baking: Footed cast iron Dutch ovens bake like your home oven, only better. You can save on cleanup by placing three canning jar rings in the bottom of a 12-inch pot, then put food to be baked on a buttered 9-inch pie plate inside the preheated pot. To bake, place a shovelful of embers below and on top of the pot. It's a dance to get cooking temperatures right, but you'll catch on with a little practice. A lid-lifter is a valuable tool to keep ashes out of your food.

Motor Picnic

Prior to the passing of Woodrow Wilson's Federal Aid Road Act of 1916, motoring on rural American roads was an adventure in muddy ruts, flat tires, gnats in the eyes and bad hairdos. With ninety percent of automobiles being "open air" models up until the late teens, motoring magazines were full of helpful advice on the question of what to wear for the motor ride as well suitable attire for tramping about the woods on a picnic.

What to Wear on a Motor Picnic

First of all, it might rain. Your car needs a rain apron like this practical version found in the September, 1904 issue of *Motor Magazine*.

And then there is the problem of dusty, mussed-up hair .....

Sensational Invention.

THE MICHEL MOTOR HAT
FOR LADIES

The only chic, dressy, rainproof head and hair protecting and light weight

Automobile Hat

The hats are made of rubber-coated Tafeta silk in leading colors

THE NEW MUSHROOM HAT WITH CURTAIN

TO DEFY DUST AND RAIN

Motor Girls

Even though early 20th century automobile outings appealed equally to both men and women, magazines such as *Motor World, Motor Magazine, Motor Camper & Tourist* were rife with stories and suggestions for the motor girl. According to *Motor Magazine's* June, 1905 issue, "Motor picnics this summer are to be all the go. The motor girl will be steering her motor car over hill and dale, and letting the breezes paint roses on her bonnie cheeks."

Motor Picnic

Manifold Cooking, 1924

One of my favorite geeky pastimes is perusing vintage science and technology magazines such as *Electrical Experimenter, Popular Mechanics, Popular Science* and *Science and Invention*. Not only do the covers sport fantastic colorful graphics, you can learn lots of new and important skills like how to cook hot dogs on an automobile exhaust manifold cooker.

"The manifold stove is new. It fits beneath the hood over the exhaust manifold of the automobile engine and may be used for baking potatoes, heating canned goods and water."
~Popular Science, May 1918

May Southworth suggests in her 1923 *Motorist's Luncheon Book* that, "There are certain makes of machines where the heat from the exhaust manifold can be utilized en route for foods hermetically sealed. Canned beans, tamales, chili con carne, chicken and many other substantials can be packed in with the engine and kept hot or heated on the way with no danger of taint from the gasoline."

While the automobile hot dog is a compelling concept, maybe we should stick with a simple motor hamper picnic like this one found in the June, 1905 edition of *Motor Magazine*.

"The motor hamper is packed with brown bread sandwiches with cream cheese & olive spread, stuffed eggs, crisp celery stalks, Rhine wine and tea punch with Jamaica rum."

A WICKER MOTOR HAMPER IN USE

Tin Can Stove Cooking

There are seemingly endless varieties of portable campstoves available for purchase today, but we make-doers get a kick out of crafting our own from whatever we can find on hand. Tin can stoves have delighted campers, hobos, and Boy & Girl Scouts for generations. I've included recipes here and there in this book for fun foods you can cook on your little rocket or other tin can stove. Here are a few other suggestions you might find useful.

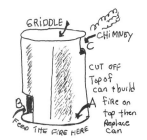

GRIDDLE

CHIMNEY

CUT OFF
Top of
can t build
A fire on
top then
Replace
can

FEED THE FIRE HERE

A Few Tips

Before lighting your little stove, be sure that you've cleared away all combustibles and that it sits on a level surface.

Any saucepan will do for cooking, but I prefer vintage copper bottom pans (Revere Ware) and they're easily found at thrift stores.

Store your little stove in an antique metal picnic basket along with a tiny cast iron frying pan, wee saucepan, waxed paper squares, tinder, and matches. Include a little bottle of olive oil, herbed garlic salt, spatula, wooden spoon, a couple enamel cups and plates and utensils and you are ready for a wanderer's lunch!

Let's Skillet-Cook on a Tin Can Stove

Fried Squash Blossoms: Use a small skillet or a flat cast iron griddle. Remove stamens and any bugs from flowers. Stuff with a dab of chevre or other cheese and herbs. Pan-fry in butter or olive oil.

Raise Chickens? Fry up a fresh-plucked egg with garden herbs.

Farinata Pancakes: Combine ½ cup garbanzo bean flour with 2 cups water in a quart jar and let sit overnight in the fridge. Into a hot skillet, drizzle olive oil and pour in a little garbanzo bean batter. Sprinkle with chopped fresh rosemary, pepper and coarse salt. Flip when browned just as you would a pancake. Eat hot from the pan as-is or top with chopped tomato. Lovely for breakfast with salt, pepper, and a little drizzle of maple syrup.

Corn on the cob cooks on a tin can rocket stove

Resources

H ere's a small smattering of mail-order sources and additional information for some of the picnic foods and equipment mentioned in this book. If you have other suggestions, contact me and I'll include your ideas, either on my website or in future editions of this book.

Bean-hole Beans and Festivals:

The Patten Lumbermen's Museum annual bean hole dinner is held the second Saturday in August in Patten, ME
> www.lumbermensmuseum.org (207)528-2650

Bean Hole Days annual festival, held mid-July in Pequot Lakes, MN
> www.pequotlakes.com (800)450-2838

Heirloom bean-hole beans are available by mail from
> *Green Thumb Farms* www. greenthumbfarms.com
> *Osborne Family Farm* www.osbornefamilyfarm.com
> *Freedom Bean Company* www.mainedrybeans.com

Pepperoni Rolls:

Tomaro's Bakery, Clarksburg, WV www.tomarosbakery.com
> Mail Order: www.annasofglenelk.com 304-566-9098

Oliverio's Italian Peppers in tomato sauce for pepperoni rolls, also made in Clarksburg, WV www.oliveriopeppers.us and select stores throughout the USA

Cast Iron Pans for live fire cooking:

Lodge Manufacturing Company makes new ironwear including Dutch ovens, footed camp Dutch ovens and iron cornstick pans
> www.lodgemfg.com

Seek out vintage cast iron in good condition that will last forever from eBay, Etsy, antique stores, yard sales, and online purveyors.

Portable Camp Ovens:

Coleman Camp Ovens are similar to the vintage portable ovens discussed on page 7, but are designed to be used with Coleman campstoves.

Vintage Calico Feedsacks:

Beginning in the 1920s, feed and flour mills started replacing their white cotton feedsacks with those made from fabulous printed designs. Yesterday's farmwives were keen on these sturdy, colorful cottons and sewed them into clothing, quilts, table linens, aprons, curtains and more. Grab them when you find them from estate sales and antique shops. The patterns from the 1930s and early 40s are my favorites.

Bibliography

American Cookery, June 1920
American Boy Book of Camplore & Woodcraft, Dan Beard, 1882
Camp Fire Cookery for Camp Fire Girls, Kellogg Co., 1930s
Camp Cookery, Horace Kephart, 1910
Economical Cookery, Marion Harris Neil, 1918
Household Arts for Home & School, Cooley & Spoor, 1921
Just You, Elizabeth Gordon, 1912
Motor Magazine, June, September 1905
One Hundred Picnic Suggestions, Linda Hall Larned, 1915
Outdoor Cookery, WV 4-H clubs, 1930s
Popular Mechanics, August, 1922, October 1948
Popular Science, May 1918
'Mongst Miners & Mines, J. C. Burrow and W. Thomas, 1895
When Mother Lets Us Cook, Constance Johnson, 1908
Suburban Life, July 1911
The Adventures of a Woman Hobo, Ethel Lynn, 1917
The Calendar of Sandwiches & Beverages, Elizabeth O. Hiller, 1922
The Motorist's Luncheon Book, May E. Southworth, 1923
Up-to-date Sandwich Book, Eva Greene Fuller, 1909

Thanks!

Thanks to all of you who joined in the picnic fun this year. Steve Millard designed the spiffy cover. Copy editors included Janet Swell, Mark Wingate and Pam Budd. Jennifer Thomas is my trusty recipe editor. Many thanks to the Monday Night Picnic Club which included Pam Budd, Annie Erbsen, Mary Lou Surgi, Jennifer Thomas, Martha Vining and many guests. You ladies were very patient with my never-ending photo-snapping. Other picnickers included Stefanie Anderson, Gianluca De Bacco, Rita Erbsen, Wes Erbsen, Laura Swell and Leon Swell. David Wright and Wayne Erbsen helped with rocket stove design. Rita Buillet from Aosta, Italy contributed her brown butter-making technique. And our office staff wins the prize for incessant pop-up picnic requests and taste-testing – Annie Erbsen, Andy Bissell, Parker Johnson and Kelli Stewart. A few of the many, and I do mean many other taste-testers included Kathy McGuigan, Marti Otto, Richard Renfro, Renate Rikkers, Neil Thomas, Lila Swell, Courtney Carriveau, Sara Webb and Dudley Wilson. And to Wayne Erbsen, my husband, publisher and picnic pal, I would like to say *"Yes, that's a homemade apple crumble-topped pie for you in the wicker picnic basket!"*

Recipe Index

>※< ≪— >※< ≪— >※< ≪— >※< ≪— >※< ≪— >※<

Native Ground Music

MORE HISTORIC COOKBOOKS BY BARBARA SWELL:

Aunt Barb's Bread Book
A Garden Supper Tonight
The First American Cookie Lady
The Lost Art of Pie Making Made Easy
Old-Time Farmhouse Cooking
Secrets of the Great Old-Timey Cooks
Mama's in the Kitchen
Children at the Hearth
Take Two and Butter 'Em While They're Hot!
Log Cabin Cooking

BOOKS OF SONGS, LORE & COOKING:

Backpocket Bluegrass Songbook
Backpocket Old-Time Songbook
Cowboy Songs, Jokes & Lingo
Front Porch Songs & Stories
Log Cabin Pioneers
Early American Cookery

Bluegrass Gospel Songbook
Outlaw Ballads & Lore
Railroad Fever
Songs of the Civil War
Rural Roots of Bluegrass
Pioneer Village Cookbook

MUSIC INSTRUCTION BOOKS:

Bluegrass Banjo for the Complete Ignoramus
Ukulele for the Complete Ignoramus
Clawhammer Banjo for the Complete Ignoramus
Bluegrass Mandolin for the Complete Ignoramus
Flatpicking Guitar for the Complete Ignoramus
Old-Time Fiddle for the Complete Ignoramus
Bluegrass Jamming on Banjo
Bluegrass Jamming on Fiddle
Bluegrass Jamming on Mandolin
Southern Mountain Instruction Books:
Banjo, Fiddle, Guitar, Mandolin and Dulcimer

FOR A FREE CATALOG, CONTACT US AT:

Native Ground Books & Music
109 Bell Road, Asheville, NC 28805
(800) 752-2656
www.nativeground.com   banjo@nativeground.com

BARBARA'S WEBSITE & BLOG:
www.logcabincooking.com